WHY

I0157667

...Us against God?

Psalm 2:1

"Why do the nations conspire and the peoples plot in vain?"

by Monica M Rohrer

Dedicated to Jesus who...

...is perfect
...is the Son of God
...heals and forgives us
...has risen from the dead
...truly loves us unconditionally
...offers us the truth and eternal life
...can give us a life of true purpose
...had come to teach us
...had suffered to free us

Index

"Foretold by the prophets,
one MAN was born,
a stable was His nursery
a manger His cradle

In a mere three years
He changed the world.
Instead of weapons,
He chose Love.

And to this day
He changes lives
and His unfailing love for us
lives on forever and ever."

(Monica 2015)

Prologue

~ A New Beginning ~
...and the End of the Old

Jesus said, "Father, forgive them, for they do not know what they are doing."

Luke 23:24 (NIV)

Why and how do I read this book?

Ever wanted to know more about God? Not sure with whom you can best talk to? You may not feel comfortable visiting a church or being 'Bible bashed' by so called 'professional Christians'. They may seem a bit too intense, but they do mean well. They are excited and their deep desire after all, is to help others to experience the way in which God can change lives for the better. It is not easy to know what a person may be seeking or where they are at, nor how to converse in the appropriate manner.

Whatever you are trying to find out about God is in any way going to be a mite difficult. So, why jump in at the deep end when you can test the water first?

This book allows you the opportunity to do just that. Here you get to hear a bit of everything. You choose which chapter you want to read. There is no specific order, other than the one that feels right for you.

"Why Us against God?" is meant for anyone with an open mind, ready to start looking for answers to some deeper questions. They may not all be answered for you, but this book will certainly assist you in your quest of finding your own purpose and peace in your life. It does not intend to concentrate on scientific and historical facts or to delve too deeply into each topic. Its aim is to address focal points in relation to God, Creation, Jesus, and ways of how you fit into all of this. The root purpose of this book is meant to expand your mind to a broader view, shed light into areas that are uncertain and to find answers for some of your questions.

This book is meant to be a catalyst for readers to go on their personal journey of discovering themselves and what part God plays in their life. We need to ask ourselves how much longer we can afford to remain ignorant, which is a question that relates to the entire humanity.

I know that God has put in my heart to write this book and pray that it will reach all the readers whom He has already chosen. Whoever and wherever you are, I pray that at the right time, you will find this book or that it will find you.

You may also act as 'courier' and pass it on to a friend. God works in mysterious ways...*His* ways.

In essence, God desires for you to know that:

- He exists
- He is real
- He is eternal
- He loves you unconditionally
- He wants you to get to know Him
- He waits for you to have faith in Him

As you journey through the chapters you will get to understand His Word in a refreshed way. The wide selection of Bible verses from the Old and New Testament demonstrate:

1. *That the principles of life have not changed since the beginning of time.*

2. *The Bible is authentic and we can trust its contents to be true*

3. *The doctrines of the Bible are still relevant to this day*

Every chapter is accompanied by corresponding Bible verses that underline and validate the messages.

Approximately 40 different authors, going back thousands of years, have written the Bible. It is not a single book but a collection of 66 books, divided in two sections, the Old Testament (BC) and the New Testament (AD).

The language would have changed in the meantime, but still bears the same relevance and importance today.

Apart from the language and time, we also need to take into account that the scenes are set in the Middle East with different customs. For instance, we may not "tear our rope", "put ash on our head" and "wear sack cloths" when we are in despair, pain or grieve. Instead, we grab anti-depressants, have a drink or two to subdue the pain, talk to a psychiatrist or kick the door.

We surely do not worry about increasing the size of our flocks of sheep and pitch our tents surrounded by olive and fig trees. These days we live in cities and worry about how we can manage to pay off our mortgage, support our families and make enough money for our retirement. Other than the setting, nothing has really changed.

Before we head off and start to unpack the chapters, I would like to give you a brief run down of how I have structured them first. Each one approaches various aspects of life - with or without God. They all open with a question, followed by a viewpoint on life in the 21st century, which then connects to Christian and biblical perspectives. Many of the chapters include personal experiences and stories to which you may be able to relate to. I pray that the poems and prayers will capture your heart.

Most likely, you would have been wondering about the significance of the apple on the cover of the book. The core of the apple represents the answers to the big questions we all have. Only, we cannot make them out through the skin. So we begin to bite or cut into the apple to get to the bottom of it. No matter from where we start digging our teeth into, we will always end up at the very same core.

Each bite or slice symbolises a chapter. Bit by bit you will get closer to the core. It will ultimately lead to **God**, who is the very **Core** of our existence and the answer to all our questions.

The Apple

What does your apple look like? What is it that you are seeking to get answers to? Are they questions such as these?

- What is the meaning of MY life?
- Do I have a choice?
- Who am I or who am I supposed to be?
- Is there a God or are we alone?
- Do I need God?
- What is it that I need to do?
- Where will I end up when I die?
- Is there life after death?

These are BIG questions, questions that have been asked since the beginning of time.

Now is the time to chose where you want to start 'biting into your apple'. Follow your heart and pick whichever chapter feels right for you. There is no set order that you need to follow, other than your very own. They all end up pointing to the Core - God. The index will lead you to your very first 'bite'.

Let's get started and see what questions will be answered as we go along together on our journey of unraveling the biggest mystery to humankind: GOD

Index

Why God's Ways

Why the Bible

Epilogue

Why us against God?

1 Why do the nations conspire
and the peoples plot in vain?
2 The kings of the Earth rise up
and the rulers band together
against the Lord and against his anointed, saying,
3 "Let us break their chains
and throw off their shackles."

Psalm 2:1-3 (NIV)

I came across these verses during my Bible reading plan, months after I commenced with my writing. When I read them the first time, it took me by surprise. This passage irrefutably captures the title and the central theme of this book at its very core. It reaffirmed that the content of this book will speak to a broad spectrum of readers. And yes, I truly believe that God wanted me to know that.

What has changed since *Psalm 2:1-3* was written? Humankind still conspires against God. Only, we don't seem to take notice or have grown indifferent. Wherever we look, God is systematically being 'removed', from educational systems to sociological environments right across 'modern' lifestyle and laws. Has God become an offence? Is it that we don't need God anymore?

Looking at the verses, what shackles do we need to throw off exactly? Is God a shackle, a bondage that keeps us from having a "great and carefree" life? In addition, what exactly would one expect a "great and carefree" life to be? Is it to chase and focus ones attention on external pleasures, riches or fame? Is this the meaning of life? Is this all we can expect from life? Then what? What happens when we reach the end of the road?

This is what happens:

> 13 Then they cried to the Lord in their trouble,
> and he saved them from their distress.
> 14 He brought them out of darkness,
> the utter darkness,
> and broke away their chains.
> Psalm 107:13-14 (NIV)

...then it continues on:

> 15 Let them give thanks to the Lord for his unfailing love
> and his wonderful deeds for mankind,
> 16 for he breaks down gates of bronze
> and cuts through bars of iron.
> Psalm 107:15-16 (NIV)

To be saved from ourselves and from our own self-deceptions, humankind will ultimately have to turn TOWARDS, rather than AGAINST God. We need to peel off all the superficial distractions of our worldly acquisitions and start to realise that seeking refuge in addictive activities and substances will not take us to eternal happiness. Could all these represent the real shackles and chains that we need to free ourselves from? If we continue to be distracted by the superficial glitz and glamour of the world, one needs to ask where all this will lead to. Will the road end here?

Why "*WHY - Us against God*"? What made me choose a title like this? Against God, really? Am I really against God or am I just not sure about the whole 'God thing'? We all have questions about life, Creation and God. We don't have the answers, but God has. One tends to take the easy road and turn away from things that cannot be explained.

"*Us against God*", is it a question or a statement? On the

other hand, could it reflect the state we find our world to be in? Can this world continue to respond to God in such a manner? Can we really afford to say, this is not for me? The main reason I was inspired to write this book was due to responses such as these from people around me.

This book may present you with an opportunity to reflect on where you currently are at; based on what you can discover for yourself throughout the chapters. So far, what kind of views and impressions have you arrived at, concerning your own understanding of God? Is it derived from what you have heard from other people, what you may have read, through your own experience or maybe there hasn't been the right moment for you yet? Some of you may even have doubts that God exists.

Perhaps you may feel that now is the right time for you to gain a clearer picture of God. This book may change your perception of who God really is and what it implies to you. I pray that this book may turn you towards God and change your life the way God has changed mine. Most importantly, that you will form your own opinion drawn from your own conclusions and what it is you will decide to do after reading this book. It will determine which direction you will be choosing.

In effect, there are only two choices, either with or without God. There really is nothing in between. When the sun casts a shadow, there too is a distinct line. It does not gradually flow into the shadow. There is no transition space in between, no grey areas. A decision has to be made at some point. We cannot negotiate a compromise. It is a rather confronting statement, but one that needs to be seriously faced. Our current global state in itself is raising this very subject. Everyday we hear on the news how this world is slowly on the decline, giving way to the dark side. This may be the reason why you are holding this book in your hands right now, looking for answers.

So why shouldn't I write and talk about God? Why do people get uncomfortable when they hear the word *GOD*? What has He done to deserve such a reaction? At some point, we all were told never to talk about politics and religion. Right?

But I'm not talking about religion; I'm talking about God, our Creator. God is not a religion. Religion is man made.

God is the One who loves all of us, regardless of our background. The One who made us the way we are, in His image. We are the pinnacle of His Creation. He is the One who gave us our special talents and abilities. God has bestowed upon us the gift of life. Why then do we still turn away from God? Why do the shutters go down as soon as the word *God* or *Jesus* is spoken aloud? Why is it acceptable to put up Buddha pictures and figurines anywhere, but a picture of Jesus is confronting and not in order? We can find the image of Buddha anywhere in the western world in public places such as shops, restaurants or show rooms. No offence intended, I have only used this as an example because everyone is familiar with Buddha. Of course there are many other images and statues on display. I once threw in the question at work when a big canvas of Buddha was hung up as a decoration. What would happen, I asked, if we were to hang up a cross or a picture of Jesus? There was not much of a reaction, as expected, but I couldn't help myself. I guess it gave me an opportunity to mention the name of Jesus.

I don't mean to cause any indignation by this example; I know Buddha was a very good and wise man and taught people a very self aware and righteous way of life. He certainly was a very peaceful and just man. But we have to keep in mind that he was only a man, he was not God. People follow and pray to him, rather than to his Creator. It appears that it is easier for people to believe and follow earthly things rather than the unseen. In Chapter "Why Faith" you will get to explore this further.

Today it seems that the Old Testament is being repeated all over again. The masses follow worldly things such as wealth, power and fame. They listen to fortunetellers and love and adore mere human idols and acquisitions.

The following verses from the first Two Commandments capture what happens when we turn away from God:

3 "You shall have no other gods before me.
4 "You shall not make for yourself an image in the form of
anything in heaven above or on the Earth beneath or in the
waters below.
5 You shall not bow down to them or worship them; for I, the
LORD your God, am a jealous God, punishing the children for
the sin of the parents to the third and fourth generation of
those who hate me,
6 but showing love to a thousand generations of those who
love me and keep my commandments.
Exodus 20:3-6 (NIV)

As we read these words, they may sound a bit out of date. Read the passages again. Is the meaning out of date? People these days have no time (they think) to reflect on God. They are ever so busy chasing the next dollar or embarking on the next adventure. Has anything really changed since? Instead of worshiping God, the Israelites idolised a 'Golden Cow'. Today we still idolise a golden cow, but in form of money, power and fame.

When we take a closer look, it begins to take on a reality that concerns us all today. We allow ourselves to be enslaved by worldly things. We love money, we aspire to be famous like a movie star or we are in pursuit of power. We believe that being rich and famous will lead to the '…and lived happily ever after'. But then again, there is always that one more thing we must have to be happy.

We are consumed by chasing after the end of the rainbow, the pot of gold, which holds the key to everlasting happiness, so we think. Instead of <u>us using money</u> or power, unfortunately it is <u>us that are being used by it</u>. There is no such thing as 'happily ever after'. Life is meant to be lived. There will always be roads that tend to take different and unexpected turns. Our conduct <u>will</u> bear consequences for generations to come. Many of these consequences are unfolding before our very eyes right now: global turmoil, wars, epidemics, religious fanaticism and an increase of natural disasters.

So, why are we against God? Is it because of bad experiences? Maybe prayers weren't answered? Might it be that misleading media headlines disillusions us? Is the existence of God too complex to believe? Are we too busy? Why is it that some people cannot accept the existence of God? Why doesn't everyone believe in Jesus? Why have so many humans doubted and rejected Jesus for over 2000 years? I was amazed when I read the passages in the NT where people who were possessed by demons confronted Jesus. At every such occasion these demons recognised Jesus instantly, they knew who He was and lashed out in total fear of Him.

21 They went to Capernaum, and when the Sabbath came, Jesus went into the synagogue and began to teach.
22 The people were amazed at his teaching, because he taught them as one who had authority, not as the teachers of the law.
23 Just then a man in their synagogue who was possessed by an impure spirit cried out,
24 "What do you want with us, Jesus of Nazareth? Have you come to destroy us? **I know who you are—the Holy One of God!"**
Mark 1:21-24 (NIV)

33 The whole town gathered at the door,
34 and Jesus healed many who had various diseases. He also drove out many demons, but he would not let the demons speak because **they knew who he was**.
Mark 1:33-34 (NIV)

Whenever the impure spirits saw him, they fell down before him and cried out, **"You are the Son of God**."
Mark 3:11 (NIV)

Why is it that humans cannot see what the demons saw? Why are we against God? It is not that the demons 'believed' in

Jesus, but they 'knew' exactly who He was. Are people scared of the invisible? Are they waiting for tangible proof? God won't be sending one on demand. He gently calls you through His Holy Spirit and waits patiently for you to trust and believe in Him. Only then will He reveal Himself and you will get as much 'proof' as you need. We all seem to be a bit like the doubting apostle Thomas.

Each of the individual chapters will take you on a tour of what life is all about: God, Faith, Creation, Sin, our Universe and back to Earth, right back to you. You will encounter many new and transforming views and insights.

All of which points right back to the core of the apple…God, who seeks us

Why Faith?

Then he said to Thomas, "Put your finger here; see my hands. Reach out your hand and put it into my side. Stop doubting and believe." Thomas said to him, "My Lord and my God!" Then Jesus told him, "Because you have seen me, you have believed; blessed are those who have not seen and yet have believed."

John 20:27-29 (NIV)

Belief vs. Fact vs. Proof

To believe in something or someone is not as easy as it sounds. It does not come naturally. Like the apostle Thomas, we all are seeking for proof that can verify the facts.

It is not necessary to believe in facts. They are tangible and can therefore be proven by scientific, natural or physical laws. Is there anyone who needs to proof the law of gravity? Would you be game to jump out of a window on the 30th floor just to proof that gravity exists?

Just as oil is lighter than water when mixed together, oil will evidently float on the top. The sun always sets in the west, water will expand in size when turning to ice, ember is hotter than fire and 2x2 equals four.

On the other hand, faith and belief is all about the heart.

To believe is to put total trust (faith) in something or someone without concrete evidence.

The word *'believe'* appears 150x, *'believed'* 69x, *'believes'* 32x, *'believer'* 8x and *'belief '* 2x (NET) in the Old and New Testament.

The NT tells the story of a Pharisee who asked Jesus to give them a proof. Jesus turned around and retorted with a question instead. It clearly demonstrated their level of (dis)belief.

I'd like to point out another couple of examples by Jesus. In front of a crowd of many thousands, Jesus declares how much God loves us. He points out that God provides the grass with everything it needs to grow. Unlike us humans, grass eventually dies off; but as humans, we can expect much more, we are immortal:

> *If that is how God clothes the grass of the field, which is here today, and tomorrow is thrown into the fire, how much more will he clothe you—you of little faith!*
> *Luke 12:28 (NIV)*

In the next scenario, the apostles were in a boat with Jesus. Whilst Jesus was having a sleep, a violent storm broke out and they all got scared and woke Him up.

> *He (Jesus) replied, "You of little faith, why are you so afraid?" Then he got up and rebuked the winds and the waves, and it was completely calm.*
> *Matthew 8:26 (NIV)*

The apostles, like us, were afraid despite having God right next to them. How could anything possibly happen to them (us)?

Faith gives us the strength and confidence to know that God will never leave our side. Faith in God leads us to the truth and frees us from worldly chains.

We find that for thousands of years humans could not fully put their trust and faith into God. First the Israelites, then the Pharisees and now it is us who have lost our way and turned away from God. Unfortunately, humans are inclined to follow what they see rather than what their heart is telling them. What are we afraid of?

Find
Answers
In
The
Heart

How true! This acronym describes best what faith really is. When humans are challenged by unexpected and unexplainable circumstances without a logical explanation, they turn away in dis-belief, especially when the word God or Jesus pops up. A common reaction is that of an invisible wall being put up as a protection against the unknown. There will always be a certain group of people who shy away from a conversation about God. They rather deny the existence of God than to face a confrontation. This is what it sounds and looks like from the outside, but in fact, what is really going on inside such a person? Would not all this uncertainty result in more unease, fear and restlessness? Would it then not be wiser to embark on an 'uncomfortable' soul searching quest in order to find inner peace? Yes, deep down, what is it that we are really afraid of?

Following acronym describes what fear also stands for:

False
Evidence
Appearing
Real

What is it that makes faith so complex? This is a stimulating question. Why faith, why indeed? Faith is neither tangible, physical nor visible; therefore, the brain will not easily accept and give in to this "new" concept of an invisible God, Jesus and the Holy Spirit. In other words, it cannot detect, touch or hear God; therefore, the logical conclusion is that the information is false.

When we are faced with something new, we start to analyse it until it makes sense. We may ask others or undertake extensive research to find some proof or evidential explanations. If we fail, the brain will dismiss this new idea. The reality is that we are thinking. We are engaging our brain. The brain is the command centre and operates in a logical order. It equips us to function physically and mentally. The brain calculates the best possible strategies to survive, overcome challenges, advance and evolve.

At the physical level, the brain governs how we perceive external data: visual (see), auditory (hear), kinesthetic (touch), olfactory (smell) and gustatory (taste). The brain receives 'data' via the nervous system, evaluates and transmits signals depending on the type of stimuli. For instance, it will initiate a healing process by producing certain chemicals for our body to adjust to a change of environment or to combat viruses and bacteria. Lastly (before I get all lost in one of my favourite subjects, the human body), the brain triggers off every single muscle movement via nerve signals. Our clever brain is, unfortunately, not capable of grasping the concept of the spiritual reality. This is where the heart (soul) comes into play:

One day when I drove home after facilitating the Alpha Course at church, without notice, a very clear thought went through my mind. It all started to add up and I wanted to make sure to add this insight to this topic.

Just briefly, the Alpha Course is designed to help either new Christians or non-Christians to learn about God, Jesus, the Holy Spirit, the Bible, praying and many other facets surrounding Christianity.

A 'seasoned' Christian may often forget how difficult and confusing these topics can appear to someone new attending Alpha. Many of the questions that are being asked by the participants have given me a deeper insight to understand what people are searching for, things they have not been aware of or never have thought about before. We often have to "go back" a few steps and try to explain in different ways by asking a different line of questions.

The Alpha course opened my eyes to the fact that people engage the brain to try to absorb the new material from the different talks. Nevertheless, as time goes on, they get to experience and learn how God works. Things slowly start to shift, People begin to feel and encounter extraordinary experiences with God. This is exactly when they stop "thinking" with the brain and switch over to their hearts; they start to converse with God. They receive their answers in their own timing through feelings and a strong sense of knowing. They slowly begin to conceive the Spirit of God.

Here is another way in which we can explain the word faith. For instance, what do you do when you need to switch on the light? Will you stand in the dark, trying to figure out how the light globe works? What do you do when you want to use your microwave, TV or your car? Would you get on your computer and conduct a research on Google? But, hang on a second. Before you can proceed, wouldn't you have to analyse how the computer operates first? Once you got all that, you can move on to do further research on the car engine, how the picture appears on your TV screen and how microwaves heat up food.

Would it be that you just have faith that it works? Isn't it enough for you to KNOW when you flick the switch that the light will come on? You have no need to question the HOW.

Why then is it that we question God? Why can't we just have faith and trust that HE "works and functions" more than perfectly? The HOW ought to be as irrelevant to us as it is to know how electricity works.

"The 'gods' know nothing, they understand nothing.
They walk about in darkness;
all the foundations of the Earth are shaken.

"I said, 'You are "gods"; you are all sons of the Most High.'
But you will die like mere mortals;
you will fall like every other ruler."

Rise up, O God, judge the Earth,
for all the nations are your inheritance.
Psalm 82:5-8 (NIV)

King David is telling us that the ones, who walk in darkness, walk without God. Then he tells them that they are 'gods', referring to us being all part of God as He created us, therefore, when we believe in Him we will live on. He foretells Jesus' coming and promises eternal life to all nations, the whole world and not just the Israelites.

To be connected with God gives a completely new perspective on life and what is important. Priorities shift as our thinking changes. It transforms us and in the process, we begin to think as one: with our brain (body), heart (soul) and spirit (our higher being).

Back to my story, as I was driving home after Alpha, I was still in an elated state as I stopped to fill my car up with petrol. When I went up to pay, the man, whom I have had many conversations with on prior occasions, asked me how my "God revival stuff" was going. I said really fantastic and He replied that he thought it was good that I believed in "THAT".

God being described as THAT quite obviously hit a cord and presented me with a new opportunity to open a dialogue about God. So what was my response? I said, yes it really is great and that I was writing a book about it. He then inquired what it was all about. I told him the title of the book and explained that I felt that God had prompted me to write this book. God would see to it that it would go into the hands of anyone who needed to read the book. To my utter surprise he got genuinely interested and said that he wanted to read it; he would be the first buyer.

Here I need to add that during one of our previous chats I mentioned church. On several occasions, I tried to invite him to one of our Christmas productions and other events. He was very adamant that under no circumstances would he set foot in a church nor would he believe in God or even being interested to know about it. This explains why I was so baffled by his sudden turnaround. God works in mysterious ways...yet again. Yes, I am very hopeful that this gentleman will get to know God one day.

Trust in the Lord and do good;
dwell in the land and enjoy safe pasture.
Take delight in the Lord, and he will give you the desires of your heart.
(Psalm 37:3, 4 NIV)

Fake to Faith

Still, many questions remain although the heart has begun to resonate with God. In the beginning, for many of us faith can be in a fragile state. The brain is still looking for logical explanations. This can cause some 'new' Christians to sway. However, deep down we know that letting faith slip away would lead us off course. So how can we connect the wisdom of the heart to the mechanical brain? *Fake to Faith*. For many this can be described as the 'transition phase'. The brain slowly begins to believe spiritual facts rather than physical facts. God will make sure that it won't take too long until we will follow the heart rather than the head.

Often on a Christian journey, things can be a bit tough as one starts out searching for God. There are many situations where it can appear rather difficult to maintain faith. We are not yet able to make sense of God's ways and perspectives from where we stand at the given time. On exactly such occasions we need to firmly hold on to our faith. It is important to have a network of the right people around us for support. Stick to your faith and believe with all your heart because you know it is right. Eventually the brain will connect with your heart. The brain is not infallible and can be 'tricked' to believe the unseen. It will receive enough evidence of the presence of God as you keep on going and holding on to your faith. Eventually, the logical side of your brain will be convinced by what your heart experiences with God. So, just continue to *fake to faith* till it happens.

Keep praying and persevere with your faith; believe and know in your heart that God will always be there for you. Hang in there and give yourself the chance to continue to learn and grow. As time goes on, you will notice that your life is slowly changing. Even your family and friends will start to notice.

You may compare it to watching a replay of a sporting event. You already know which competitor or team will win. You can just kick back and enjoy without getting uptight. There is no need for you to second guess and worry, as you already know the outcome.

Unfortunately, life has no 'replay button'. Life is live. There is no second chance to rehearse and repeat. So next time you get caught up in one of life's many challenges and tribulations, don't despair and trust God. Faith in God always makes you a winner; there is no need for a 'replay button'.

Fake to Faith is better than to toss it in and ultimately drift away. I promise you that if you really desire to know God, He will make it happen. Why? Because He wants to have you in His family, He wants all of us reunited with Him. That is the endgame.

We need to focus on the future. The past cannot be changed. Only what we do now can shape our future. Every day and every second represent a new beginning. It is never too late to start all over and take a different direction. God never gives up on any of us and relentlessly gives us new opportunities. His love and support is always there for us if we are willing to accept it.   Even though we feel we have messed up, God patiently remains right there alongside of us, giving us new hope.

But you, Lord, are a compassionate and gracious God, slow to anger, abounding in love and faithfulness.
Psalm 86:15 (NIV)

If we want to communicate via the telephone or Internet, first a form of connection has to be established, either by plugging into a line or by connecting to a Wi-Fi. A brand new TV or radio needs to be tuned to the right frequencies to store and receive the available channels.

God also communicates, but He doesn't have to use any satellites, landline or antennas. His communication method is wired by love. We can only 'hear' Him if we tune into His frequency. How can we 'tune' in? Are we also equipped with an 'Auto Tuning Mode'?

Wouldn't it be so simple to just flick the switch and have God on the other side of the line? Actually, it is that simple.

The switch is called *faith* and the connection is *love* and *prayer*. Prayer establishes the communication with God.

God does not communicate with our mechanical brain, He only communicates with our heart, which is our soul. This is the purpose of His Creation. However, He has also equipped us with a perfect body so that we can live on this Earth and experience life to its fullest, with all its beauty and glory; as well as with the opposite of the ugliness of crime, brutality and injustice.

Each one of our soul holds within a small part of God and therefore we are connected with God, regardless whether we know of Him (yet) or not. This connection is a necessary part of our reality. Like God, we exist as a trinity: body, soul and spirit. All areas need to be in harmony to avoid an imbalance, which causes tension.

Prayers come in many different forms. For most people, the first thing that comes to mind is having to go to church, kneel and pray repetitive prayers that don't make sense. Guess what, if it's not coming from your heart, they will not make sense to God either.

What then is a prayer? A prayer can be a thanksgiving or expression of gratitude for all the good things that are happening in life. In a prayer, one can acknowledge the blessings that have been received such as special gifts and talents that make one stand out. A prayer can also be just like a normal conversation, having a 'chat' with God and sharing with him what you have been up to, what is bothering you or what has delighted you during the day. You can pray for other people's wellbeing or healing. When you intercede for others, your heart is in the right place and filled with love and compassion for the other person.

Since God is your Father, you can ask Him for help in any area you are struggling with. Once you make it a daily 'habit' to talk to God, you will build a relationship and God can connect with you. You will start to 'hear' him.

We are part of God and God is part of us. Therefore, God has to be part of every one's daily life and not only in troubled times. You wouldn't just get in touch with your parents or friends only when you are in need of something, would you?

Next time you go for a walk, drive to or from work, sit in the train or are just reflecting, why not 'catch up' with God too. Do this with love in your heart so that can feel the presence of God.

Once you can feel, hear and understand God, you need to respond in love and allow it to resonate within you. At this point, you have established a two-way communication. Only with the love of God in your heart will you have the strength to shield yourself from thoughts such as hatred, egoism, revenge, cruelty, disregard and jealousy. They are of total contrast to love, but yet so close. Such kind of negativity is capable of eliciting a powerful force that will inflict pain not just on others but on you also. Looking at it globally and historically, it always resulted in destruction of people and nations.

The more you turn to God the more the opposite side will try to intervene and pull you away, back to the dark side of life, evil. As long as you keep your faith in God and follow His ways, you remain safe. This all takes us back to the two commandments that Jesus was responding to when asked by the Pharisees:

> 'Love the Lord your God with all your heart
> and with all your soul and with all your mind.'
> 'Love your neighbour as yourself.'
> Matthew 22:37, 39-40 (NIV)

One night on my way home after Yoga, something peculiar happened. Driving along, my eyes fell on a neon sign in front of a church. It read: 'Come and pray'. To my surprise, I almost started to laugh because at that very instant it appeared so ridiculous to me. In my imagination, I saw all these people going to church on Sundays, kneeling down and praying. Then they would leave church with a smile. But as soon as they get home, all the good intentions are tossed aside and they get straight back to their old ways. Instead of asking the neighbour how he is or lending a hand to someone, their selfish thinking drives them to gossip, backstab and ignore other people's needs.

That night I realised that this was in fact a message from God. He was telling me how this behaviour deeply saddens him. He has to put up with these useless and deceitful lies day after day. It dawned on me; whom are people trying to impress? Going to church and acting like saints, only to return home to fall right back into their bad behaviours without a second thought. As if God would not notice, on the contrary, it is an insult. It was as if I heard God's voice telling me: **"If you _really_ want to pray and honour me, go out there and be nice to each other. Love and help people around you. When you are 'nice' to them, you are in fact nice to Me. This is how you ought to pray and truly honour and love Me!**

The story I'm sharing with you now is close and personal. I pray that it may help some of you to understand faith better.

When one gets older, the matter of dying tends to crop up. Questions, such as where am I going to end up when I close my eyes the last time, seem to stand out. For many years, it has been a scary thought for me. As mentioned in chapter 'How did I find God', I have been involved in many different types of spiritual activities such as channeling, palm reading, fortunetellers and the like.

I have always believed that that we have souls, which will move on to the spiritual domain once we die. Nevertheless, the question that daunted me was, would I be all by myself? What if I just 'floated around' somewhere in space, completely lost in this vast darkness of the unknown?

When I became a Christian, I started to pray to Jesus that He would 'pick me up' so that I don't get lost. That would comfort me to a certain degree, but it still left me troubled and uncertain.

One day, not even so long ago, for no specific reason, I started to think about it again. Then, as if a veil had been removed from my eyes, I realised how simple it all is. Firstly, *my soul will already know what to do because that is where it was 'born'. Secondly, when I got baptised 3 years ago, I confessed my faith in Jesus, welcomed Him in my life and decided that I would follow Him. From that point on, Jesus has been living in me. My realisation was that Jesus would not have to 'come and pick me up'; He is already with me now. I cannot explain the enormous relief I felt to know that Jesus would take me by my hand and carry me off to where I belong. All will be well, save and perfect. Afterwards I actually was a bit amused at myself, thinking as how long it took me to come to this (now) logical conclusion. Some of us are a bit on the slow side…*

This story shows just how faith has changed my life. Faith in Jesus has removed all my fears and uncertainties and given me the freedom to pursue my true purpose. Loneliness is no longer part of my life. My wish for all people is that they too can experience such a peaceful and liberating feeling. This is the kind of freedom that Jesus promises us.

In the NT (NIV) the word 'FREE' can be found 49 times and the word FREEDOM appears 14 times. It emphasises the importance of faith, which is truly the key that opens the door to the impossible: to enjoy life as a free spirit in this world.

Here are just some of the verses that relate to the freedom that is available to all of us:

Now the LORD is the Spirit, and where the Spirit of the LORD is, there is freedom.
2 Corinthians 3:17 (NIV)

But whoever looks intently into the perfect law that gives freedom, and continues in it—not forgetting what they have heard, but doing it—they will be blessed in what they do.
James 1:25 (NIV)

Then you will know the truth, and the truth will set you free."
John 8:32 (NIV)

because through Christ Jesus the law of the Spirit who gives life has set you free from the law of sin and death.
Romans 8:2 (NIV)

It is for freedom that Christ has set us free. Stand firm, then, and do not let yourselves be burdened again by a yoke of slavery.
Galatians 5:1 (NIV)

The amazing story of Zachariah, the father of John the Baptist, describes how faith, even for a 'God fearing' priest, can be weakened. One day, whilst burning incense in the temple, the angel Gabriel appeared to him and told him that He would get a son. Here you need to know that both, him and his wife Elizabeth were old and past childbearing age. Despite his faith, he still questioned the angel in disbelief, doubting the message of God that was delivered to him. The angel then told him that he would not be able to utter a word until the birth of his son because he had no faith. For nine long months, the poor man could not utter a single word. If you like to read the full story, you can find it in the Gospel of Luke, starting at chapter 1 verse 5 (NT).

We can also find many men and women in the Old and New Testament whose faith had never faltered. They displayed unconditional faith in the Lord and followed His ways and commandments. Their faith has turned them into heroes, of whom even many movies have been made and countless books written:

- Noah
- Abraham
- Joseph
- Moses
- Ruth
- King David

Although Hollywood gave its own spin on the events, the movies are still based on true stories of real people, who God had chosen and blessed. They all have followed God's instructions without losing faith. Despite the fact that the predicaments appeared impossible to overcome, their faith remained rock solid. They found the necessary strength and wisdom from God. In the end, all turned out exactly as God predicted it would. Faith can move mountains; or is it God that does?

Noah took on a seemingly impossible task and began to build the ark even though it did not look like it would rain. Just as God had promised, his family and all the animals survived the flood:

When the dove returned to him in the evening, there in its beak was a freshly plucked olive leaf! Then Noah knew that the water had receded from the Earth.
Genesis 8:11 (NIV)

Abraham, he (God changed his name from Abram to Abraham) left his home without knowing where he is going to end up. He simply put his trust in God and followed His call and he surly got blessed.

1 The LORD had said to Abram, "Go from your country, your people and your father's household to the land I will show you.
2 "I will make you into a great nation,
and I will bless you; I will make your name great,
and you will be a blessing.
Genesis 12:1-2 (NIV)

Joseph, without knowing what the future held for him, he stuck to his faith and endured grueling hardship. He persevered in his faith and changed people and history:

4 Then Joseph said to his brothers, "Come close to me."
*When they had done so, he said, "**I am your brother Joseph,***
the one you sold into Egypt!
5 And now, do not be distressed and do not be angry with
*yourselves for selling me here, because **it was to save lives***
***that God sent me ahead of you**. 6 For two years now there*
has been famine in the land, and for the next five years there
will be no plowing and reaping.
*7 **But God sent me ahead of you to preserve for you a***
remnant on Earth and to save your lives by a great
***deliverance**.*
*8 "So then, it was **not you who sent me here, but God**.*
Genesis 45:4-8 (NIV)

Moses, after some persuasion, freed his people of slavery and led them out of Egypt. One of the many promises made by God that was fulfilled:

And I will bring you to the land I swore with uplifted hand to
give to Abraham, to Isaac and to Jacob. I will give it to you as
a possession. I am the LORD.'"
Exodus 6:8 (NIV)

Ruth, (widowed) refused to leave her mother-in-law and insisted to stay with her. She put her faith into God, not knowing where all this would lead to. She ended up getting married again to a wonderful husband and bore him children, a biblical fairytale. This is what Ruth said to her mother in-law:

But Ruth replied, "Don't urge me to leave you or to turn back
from you. Where you go I will go, and where you stay I will
stay. Your people will be my people and your God my God.
Ruth 1:16 (NIV)

King David, he had faithfully followed God's words. He started out tending the flocks and became a powerful ruler:

*I will **walk about in freedom**, for I have sought out your*
precepts.
Psalm 119:45 (NIV)

Who else could give us such freedom? No other but the One who created all. Have faith and accept His help. Always remember that God never stops loving you, no matter how many times you may step on the wrong path. The door is always open for you to get back in. Let go and accept God's help and love.

I find the following verses one of the saddest ones:

4 Jesus said to them, "A prophet is not without honour except
in his own town, among his relatives and in his own home."
5 He could not do any miracles there, except lay his hands on
a few sick people and heal them.
6 He was amazed at their lack of faith.
Mark 6:4-6 (NIV)

Reading these verses, I can almost feel the pain that Jesus must have felt. People closest to Him, did not believe in Him. All He could do was perform miracles on a physical level. But what He really was yearning to do, was to perform miracles of spiritual healing. These are the true and faithful miracles of God.

Nevertheless, there were people who had absolute faith in Jesus. In these closing verses, a Roman centurion acted on his deep-seated faith in the power of Jesus:

5 When Jesus had entered Capernaum, a centurion came to him, asking for help.
6 "Lord," he said, "my servant lies at home paralysed, suffering terribly."
7 Jesus said to him, "Shall I come and heal him?"
8 The centurion replied, "Lord, I do not deserve to have you come under my roof. But just say the word, and my servant will be healed.
9 For I myself am a man under authority, with soldiers under me. I tell this one, 'Go,' and he goes; and that one, 'Come,' and he comes. I say to my servant, 'Do this,' and he does it."
*10 When Jesus heard this, he was amazed and said to those following him, "**Truly I tell you, I have not found anyone in Israel with such great faith**.*
Matthew 8:5-10 (NIV)

Which points right back to the core of the apple…God, who is all loving and faithful

Why God?

Who is God?

This would have been one of the most challenging chapters to get started on. It's not because I don't know what to write, the question is, where and how do I begin? In fact, is there even enough paper on Earth to contain who God is?

When I initially launched into this chapter, I was so convinced that it was going to be a breeze. Did I not read the whole Bible in 2014? Am I not excited about all of my extraordinary encounters with God? Am I not bursting with enthusiasm to share with you who God is?

Here I'm sitting with my eager fountain pen in hand, a full jar of ink ready at my side and still, I have no idea where and how to open this chapter. I am cutting, pasting and copying. Over and over again, I'm deleting everything I have written and end up back at the start. Empty pages keep glaring at me. How is it that nothing I have thought of so far can measure up to God? Everything appears so inadequate and unworthy. Had I been a reader, I'd have skipped this chapter. However, as my momentum came to a staggering halt, I began to realise that God is teaching me another lesson. I felt His immense greatness and power. I was overcome with a strong sense of humility and awe. Do we actual have earthly words that can match who God really is? How 'on Earth' can I possibly describe a supernatural Entity that created all there is?

So here I am, starting afresh, yet with an idea that finally appears to sit right. Why not start with His name first? Is it not the first thing one does when introducing someone? But then again, God is not just *someone*.

Moses was faced with the same dilemma when he was on Mount Sinai before he returned to his people with the Ten Commandments:

13 Moses said to God, "Suppose I go to the Israelites and say to them, 'The God of your fathers has sent me to you,' and they ask me, 'What is his name?' Then what shall I tell them?" 14 God said to Moses, "I AM WHO I AM. This is what you are to say to the Israelites: 'I AM has sent me to you.' "
Exodus 3:13-14 (NIV)

Variations of other versions:

"I AM THAT I AM"
"I AM WHO AM"

"I AM", is in present tense, no past, no future, just as is, as it was as it will be, timeless. The ALPHA and OMEGA, "The Beginning and The End" or "The First and The Last".

The name Yahweh (in Hebrew YHWH, they had no vowels) first appeared in verse 14 as the meaning of "I AM THAT I AM", "the unchanging, eternal, self-existent God". Now most Bible versions translate Yahweh as LORD (small capitals to express the highest possible reverence). There are other variations used beside Yahweh, such as Yehova, Yahwe, Yahveh, Yahve, Wahvey, Jahvey, Jahweh or Jehovah.

The People of Israel would not dare to say His name as it was too holy to be spoken aloud. Instead they replaced YHWH with **Adonai.** Anonai is the plural of Adon, which in old Hebrew means one endowed with absolute control. It signifies a master above all. This all indicates that people have always been in search to find the 'right' and befitting name for our Creator. At the end of the day, I am convinced that all He desires for us is to seek Him, as long as we address Him with respect. In the Bible, we find many other names by which God can be addressed, of some He used to refer to Himself:

- Father in Heaven
- LORD of all
- God Almighty
- Creator of the Heavens and Earth
- King of Kings
- LORD Almighty
- LORD God
- Sovereign LORD
- Mighty God
- Everlasting God
- Alpha and Omega
- Abba (Father in Aramaic)
- Comforter
- Most High God
- Glorious LORD
- Jehovah (Hebrew)
- King of Heaven
- King of Glory
- King of all Nations
- LORD God Almighty

The list is endless as there are many more references to God.

Now that we seem to have the introduction down pat, we can start to look at how God's character can be best described. Here are only some of God's countless attributes that occur throughout the Old and New Testament:

- Holy
- Invisible
- Infinite
- Everlasting
- Eternal
- Love
- Life
- Light
- Righteous
- Exalted
- Merciful
- Gentle
- Forgiving
- Patient
- Saving
- Guiding
- Protecting
- Faithful
- Trustworthy
- Honest
- Most powerful
- Giving His Blessings
- Giving His Grace
- Impartial
- Just
- Providing
- Majestic
- Splendorous
- Glorious
- Almighty
- Healing the body and spirit
- Perfect

...and again, the list can go on forever until the supply of paper runs out. But I'm sure you would have already come across quite a few of those in the verses you have read so far. Some of these characteristics may resonate with you and illustrate how small and dependent we really are. Truly, who is our God and what is His character?

A few years back during one of my trips to Switzerland, I encountered God's presence:

I visited a church with my family where Alan Ames gave a talk. He was born in England and now lives in Perth. He comes from a very dubious and dark past but had encountered God in a big way. It completely transformed his life and he is now travelling the world, speaking in various Catholic churches and has written several books about the Holy Spirit. At the end of his talk, everyone was invited to go up to the front. Alan then would briefly touch each person on the forehead. On occasions, a healing would occur or people would simply faint and fall backwards. I am sure you would have seen things like that on TV. In disbelief, I was watching how some people actually passed out. Being a typical skeptic, I figured that they were taking it a bit to the extreme. How could one possibly faint by only being touched for one second, or so I thought? Eventually we all proceeded to the front. I was curious if anything would happen to me too.

When Alan was about to my forehead, I closed my eyes. The moment I got touched, I understood why people fainted. I had never experienced anything like this before. It felt like I was packed in cotton wool. Everything around me felt so soft, ever so gentle, light, safe, quiet and warm. It is very difficult to describe in words. I felt myself sinking deeper into it, never wanting to leave this peaceful space. I thought I was going to fall backwards, but in the nick of time and with great regret, I came out of it. I was absolutely taken by this extraordinary experience. I would never have thought that God is so gentle. Often in the Old Testament God is sometimes described as angry, vengeful and mighty powerful which does not resonate with what I have felt. It totally changed the way I thought about God, revealed to me by His Holy Spirit. If this is what Heaven is like, I cannot wait to get there…

How can we identify ourselves with such an exalted, invisible almighty God? Can we even begin to imagine what He is like? God cannot change; He is perfect. I found that the subsequent verses express some of God's desires and characteristics:

18 The wrath of God is being revealed from heaven against all the godlessness and wickedness of people, who suppress the truth by their wickedness,
19 since what may be known about God is plain to them, because God has made it plain to them.
20 For since the Creation of the world God's invisible qualities—his eternal power and divine nature—have been clearly seen, being understood from what has been made, so that people are without excuse.
Romans 1:18-20 (NIV)

5 Then the LORD came down in the cloud and stood there with him and proclaimed his name, the LORD
6 And he passed in front of Moses, proclaiming, "The LORD, the LORD the compassionate and gracious God, slow to anger, abounding in love and faithfulness,
Exodus 34:5-6 (NIV)

In his letter, the apostle Paul tells the Roman Christians how humans choose to ignore the existence and importance of God, despite of all the evidence. People tend to justify their actions rather than to first learn and understand what is in line with God and make amends accordingly. God did not intend to make life complicated, but people still choose their own will over and above God's warnings. In fact, I concluded that life is not as hard when one acknowledges God.

The word *wrath* can evoke a rather terrifying reaction. What it really refers to, are the consequences of our denial. God cannot accept anything less of us. In order for us to be able to, one day, dwell in His heavenly dimension, we have to submit to different laws.

There is no compromise; we are either with God or not. The Chapter 'Why not sin' focuses on this topic.

Following verses in Psalm 107 are praises to God's Character and deeds. King David even reiterated the first sentence four times. The verses 8 to 16 tell us what God does for us, 21 to 32 show us how we can demonstrate our gratefulness and respect:

> 8 *Let them give thanks to the Lord for his unfailing love*
> *and his wonderful deeds for mankind,*
> *9 for he satisfies the thirsty*
> *and fills the hungry with good things.*

> 15 *Let them give thanks to the Lord for his unfailing love*
> *and his wonderful deeds for mankind,*
> *16 for he breaks down gates of bronze*
> *and cuts through bars of iron.*

> 21 *Let them give thanks to the Lord for his unfailing love*
> *and his wonderful deeds for mankind.*
> *22 Let them sacrifice thank offerings*
> *and tell of his works with songs of joy.*

> 31 *Let them give thanks to the Lord for his unfailing love*
> *and his wonderful deeds for mankind.*
> *32 Let them exalt him in the assembly of the people*
> *and praise him in the council of the elders.*
> *(NIV)*

Because of his unshakable faith, loyalty and obedience, God blessed King David in all his endeavours. All his enemies were overcome by the power of God. He passionately wanted others to know who God is and that they too can receive His blessing. God is love:

8 Whoever does not love does not know God, because God is love.
1John 4:8 (NIV)

Moreover, this experience has opened my eyes to God's tender love for ALL:

One of the ways I pray and talk to God is to appreciate nature and admire its perfect beauty and diversity. One evening I was walking in the park, observing all the different kinds of trees, pondering how many species there are on Earth. It is impossible to imagine how they all have been made from a unique mold, able to adapt to the various climates and conditions. It can be rather overwhelming to reflect on just one single part of Creation, the trees.

As I was walking past a tree, I casually stretched out my hand to get hold of one of the overhanging branches. As soon as I touched one leaf, an immense sensation overtook me by surprise.

For a brief second I sensed how God would have felt when He created the trees. He didn't just stretch His hands out and said:"…and let there be a tree." I became aware of the tender love God put into all of His Creation. It emanated through my whole being. It felt so gentle and loving. He made sure that all is beautiful, perfect and with a purpose. Tears welled up in my eyes, causing unexpected emotions to surface.

Why do humans abuse and destroy this planet? Why don't they care enough? How painful and hurtful must all this be to God? Our planet Earth, all its vegetation and animals are not our property; they are His. We therefore should treat everything around us with respect and allow for the future generations to enjoy all just as we have.

Why didn't I realise this before? I guess I never took time to really look at trees in such a way. Although I love trees so much that I cringe each time I hear a chainsaw. It is a bit like killing a living being.

During my walks, I often tend to stop and touch a trunk of a tree, but I have never felt something as overwhelming as when touching this leaf so gently. Prior to this experience, I used to imagine God with and outstretched arm, commanding: ..."and let there be...." and so it was. As it is written in Genesis:

Then God said,
"Let the land produce vegetation:
seed-bearing plants and trees on the land that bear fruit with
seed in it, according to their various kinds."
And it was so.
Genesis 1:11 (NIV)

...Just like that! The book of Genesis does not go into any specifics; it only describes the order of Creation and what God was saying. It makes it sound so instantaneous and rather unemotional.

On the contrary, there was so much more than "just" creating our Earth. Can we ever really understand it? Could it be that God created Earth because He was bored and had nothing better to do? Or maybe there really is a Grand Plan, which we cannot possibly fathom.

A few months ago, a fascinating notion transpired: Could Earth, with its incredible diversity, breathtaking beauty and absolute perfection, be the reflection of God's image and character? A canvas of an infinite pallet of exquisite colours, temperatures that can either freeze or sore to high intensity, contrasting landscapes, a powerful nature that makes us feel small and helpless at times, devastating hurricanes and cyclones, rain that can either cause floods or provide precious and life-giving water, unbearable droughts but necessary to keep the balance, vast oceans and sweeping deserts that appear to go on forever, mountain peaks so high that they are hidden by the clouds and valleys with rivers streaming down. The Earth is a most amazing planet with an everlasting cycle of life. Even observed from space, our blue planet is incomparable to all the other planets.

Like God, the Earth provides for everything that is needed to live, with seemingly countless facets that are all intertwined. To make life possible, every atom, microorganism, bacteria, DNA and any other 'micros' are interconnected.

Is the Earth what God 'looks' like? Does our World reflect God's personality? Earth functions according to set natural laws, therefore is as predictable as God is. Certain conditions evoke certain outcomes and reaction. For instance, a hurricane does not just happen unexpectedly. It can only happen when the correct conditions are present. Nothing can just be triggered off by accident.

For anything to exist and co-exist in harmony, both physically and spiritually, there have to be very specific rules and laws in place. The same would apply to us humans but we seem to make up our own rules and regulations according to our personal benefit and comfort, often disregarding how it affects the environment.

Everything that encompasses Creation is interlinked, not just us and our planet Earth, but also other star systems, galaxies and universes containing planets, moons and stars. Without the sun or the moon, any life form on our planet would be unable to sustain. Without the exact position of the planets spinning around, the Earth wouldn't even exist. Just like our Creator, the universe remains a perfect mystery. Our advanced technology and science will never suffice to unlock the ultimate secret of the beginning of all there is; nor are we destined to in this lifetime.

Often I ask people who do not believe in God this question: Have you ever wondered why Earth has never been hit by an asteroid or comet, big enough to destroy and wipe out all there is? How many millions of years has Earth been around without any fatal collisions? What or who keeps us safe? Who is watching over us? There really can only be one answer.

Let us zero in on the incredibly complex Human anatomy; could we actually call it a universe in itself? Each cell and organ, the nervous, lymphatic, muscular, skeletal, digestive, respiratory, reproductive, endocrine and vascular systems are required to be fully integrated in order to function as a whole.

One starts to realise what it really means when the Bible tells us that we are created in our Creator's image.

So God created mankind in his own image,
in the image of God he created them;
male and female he created them.
Genesis 1:27 (NIV)

It all connects; the body with the mind, the mind with the spirit and the spirit with our Creator. In short, no living being, may it be human, animal or plant could exist in the absence of perfection.   .

In view of all this, God is in everything. God has created all and 'runs' it all. I believe if God were to 'pull the plug' and turn away, nothing would be able to neither live nor procreate anymore. No seed would germinate and no soil would be fertile. There simply would be no *breath of life* anywhere. God is both, the Creator and Source of all life.

When you hear the saying *to be in a relationship with God*, it may at first sound a bit strange. Nevertheless, this relationship is absolutely necessary since we are a part of Him. He is our 'power source' to which we need to be plugged in.

So how do we stay 'plugged' in? Jesus tells us 'to pray'. Apart from reading the Word of God in the Bible, prayer plays the main part of being connected with God. We can give thanks, ask for His help for self or others or just talk. We can feel His presence and draw strength and wisdom from His energy.

The book of Revelation describes how God is being constantly worshipped and revered in the heavenly realm. Even in God's Kingdom, everyone is in need of God:

11 All the angels were standing around the throne and around
the elders and the four living creatures. They fell down on their
faces before the throne and worshiped God,
12 saying:
"Amen!
Praise and glory
and wisdom and thanks and honour

and power and strength
be to our God for ever and ever.
Amen!"
Revelation 7:11-12 (NIV)

It truly signifies the greatness of our God and the unmatched and everlasting power of His presence. Unlike these elders, praying face down, how do we demonstrate our gratitude, love and reverence to God here on Earth?

The moment we re-unite with our Creator, we will realise who God truly is. I think we too will go face down, but with shame and regret, realising that our perception of God truly missed the mark. Neither does *in His image* mean that God has a physical body that looks like the human physiology.

But both, God and humans are one in three, a Trinity: Father/mind, Son/body and Holy Spirit/spirit-soul. *In His image,* also means that He has equipped us with absolutely everything we need to become pure like Him in spirit. Our DNA encapsulates the whole universe, with endless possibilities.

There is only one little three-letter word that stands between the majority of humans to access that awesome power, power that is pure and perfect love: *Sin*. But later on, we get to read more about sin in the chapter 'Why not sin'. It draws a clearer picture of its meaning and repercussions.

Nowhere in the Bible can we find a description of what God looks like. In the Old Testament, Ezekiel describes how he saw God in *His Glory*. In Exodus, God manifests as the burning bush to speak to Moses. God led the Israelites out of Egypt. At night, he appeared in form of fire and during the day as a cloud of smoke. We also read that God would reveal His presence by a cloud hovering over the Ark of the Covenant.

The second Commandment tells us not to worship any kind of image (nor anything in heaven above). Apart of idolatry, it also indicates that we should not have an image of Him. It does not bear any importance to our existence.

*4 "You shall not make for yourself an image in the form **of***
***anything in heaven above** or on the Earth beneath or in the*
waters below.
5 You shall not bow down to them or worship them;
Gen 20:4 (NIV)

It has even been repeated in the New Testament that we ought to refrain from seeking and making up an image of God. By doing so, we would only idolise a man-made object and deviate from what God clearly wants for us; to connect and love Him with our hearts so that we can feel His immense and pure energy.

"Therefore since we are God's offspring, we should not think
that the divine being is like gold or silver or stone—an image
made by human design and skill
Acts 17:29 (NIV)

and this is why:

15 The idols of the nations are silver and gold,
made by human hands.
16 They have mouths, but cannot speak,
eyes, but cannot see.
17 They have ears, but cannot hear,
nor is there breath in their mouths.
18 Those who make them will be like them,
and so will all who trust in them.
Psalm 135:15-18 (NIV)

In the OT, God is also described as a jealous God.

Do not worship any other god, for the LORD, whose name is
Jealous, is a jealous God.
Exodus 34:14 (NIV)

I felt that this point might be important to cover, as it is often misunderstood. This happens when one only reads a part of the verses rather than considering the whole context.

Initially, I could not quite make sense of why God would be described as being jealous. What does this mean? It sounds too 'human', not at all like the all knowing, most exalted God and Creator of all. Why would God have to be jealous? He tells us to love Him above anything else. Doesn't it rather sound a bit over the top? It appears to conflict with the image of a loving, gentle and caring God. Is this a contradiction concerning God? Or is He telling us that He really is the endgame, anything else is like chasing after the wind (King Solomon's sayings in Ecclesiastes, OT). Does He want to warn us that anything else will with guarantee lead to a *dead*-end?

In the OT, we can find the word *jealous* 19 times (New International Version). Each one relates to God's character. *Jealousy is mentioned* 8 times. The New Testament only mentions the word twice:

Or do you think Scripture says without reason that he jealously longs for the spirit he has caused to dwell in us?
James 4:5 (NIV)

and

21 You cannot drink the cup of the Lord and the cup of demons too; you cannot have a part in both the Lord's table and the table of demons.
22 Are we trying to arouse the Lord's jealousy? Are we stronger than he?
1Corinthians 10:21-22 (NIV)

These verses from the New Testament explain what is truly meant by describing our God as a jealous God.

By James: His deepest desire is to be with us (to dwell in us)

By Paul: If we were to follow anything else but Him, it could only lead to destruction. One cannot serve two masters. There really are only two choices, which have to be made at some point in time.

The authors for the OT used this expression to make sure people understood the severity of the message, whereas the authors of the NT had no further need because of the teachings and examples of Jesus.

Which points right back to the core of the apple…God, the Creator, unmatched in power; the Source of all life

Where is God?

For this is what the high and exalted One says—
he who lives forever, whose name is holy:
"I live in a high and holy place,

Isaiah 57:15 (NIV)

Spoken by Jesus:
"This, then, is how you should pray:
" 'Our Father in heaven,
hallowed be your name
Matthew 6:9 (NIV)

King Solomon's prayer:
Hear from heaven, your dwelling place,
1 Kings 8: 30 (part of) (NIV)

A prayer from Moses:
Look down from heaven, your holy dwelling place
Deuteronomy 26:15 (part of) (NIV)

Now that we have been formerly introduced, we want to find out where God really is. Where does He dwell? What we refer to as *Heaven* is the representation of the spiritual dominion. As humans, we need some sort of physical image to relate to. That is why, when we pray, we often gaze up to the sky, the heavens. Maybe it is with a small hope of seeing God somewhere in the clouds. God is so immense and indescribable that He dwells in everything. All is part of Him. God exists outside the time and space domain. He can see the past, present and future all at the same instant.

Shortly before my Baptism on 24 April 2011, the dots started to connect. As I was walking my dog, my heart started to pound and I knew that God had put a thought in my mind. Everything made perfect sense. God actually lives in people, not around us. Neither does He dwell in a building called church. God resides in each one of us, if we wish so. We are His church and He waits for us to invite Him in. As Luke writes in Acts "...He is not far from any of us." We don't need to shout, a quiet sincere and loving prayer is enough for Him.

I was deeply touched because until that time it hadn't occurred to me. It was a new revelation. Just as my faith and understanding grew, so did my understanding. God would have patiently waited for me to catch up. But I did eventually; everyone in their own time. I am glad I heard Jesus knock on my door. I have not looked back since I opened the door for Him. I can hardly believe I made it this far without Him:

"Here I am! I stand at the door and knock. If anyone hears my voice and opens the door, I will come in and eat with that person, and they with me."
Revelation 3:20 (NIV)

God did this so that they would seek him and perhaps reach out for him and find him, though he is not far from any one of us
Acts 17:27 (NIV)

In conjunction with our Baptism, the church asked us to write a testimony that we can read in front of the congregation. I procrastinated until 4 days before, which happened to be Easter Sunday. I couldn't think of anything interesting to write. My story was not as exciting compared to what others had experienced. I had no earthmoving encounter with Jesus to speak of. It all happened gradually, like putting together a puzzle with thousands of pieces. Working on the puzzle everyday would not show much of a change, but in time, the true picture would start to emerge. You wouldn't be able to write a gripping story about that either. What truly counts is what happens on the inside and the journey itself.

Anyway, I kept praying to God to help me put together a testimony that would have some sort of impact for others who were considering to get baptised. So, with only four nights to go, it dawned on me that God cannot help and guide me unless I grab a pen and start writing. With that in mind, I sat on my bed (with my tablet) and started my 'boring' story. Hello, my name is …and I am from…I've been going to church since… etc.

Only a few sentences into it, something unexpected happened. My writing style began to transform into a poem. I was astounded and continued on. I felt like my hand and mind was guided. At the end, it only took a few minor changes and this poem came to life:

Today, on this Easter day
You have washed away my sins

My heart is open and ready
To welcome You my Lord
As I ask you to reside in my heart

For this is your home
For this is your church
For now, for ever, since the beginning of time

This is where You, my Father want to be
This is where You fill my life with your love

As I will follow Your son Jesus
As I will follow Your will in faith

Amen

20.04.2011

At my Baptism, I knew that this was what God wanted people to hear. There was no need for anything else for me to recount. Yes, God is everywhere; we only have to call His name in faith and love.

Which points right back to the core of the apple…God, who dwells in us

Is God and the Bible just a Lie?

So far, we have learned who God is by His name, character, appearance and where He resides. Let us take it a step back and try another direction by asking this question: Could this all be just a lie? If we were to insist that there is no God, we then also had to argue that the whole Bible is a lie. Could this be the biggest lie since the beginning of time?

Every single author whose work is represented in the Bible would have had to come up with some rather 'colourful fantasy' stories. All prophecies would only be a fiction of someone's imagination. Then we would have to ask ourselves how hundreds of prophesies in the OT were fulfilled in the NT. The NT was written hundreds of years later and around 50 years after the death of Jesus and the message remained consistent. The constitutions and justice systems of countries are built on the values of the Bible to the present time.

In addition, Jesus was born and renewed the covenant to re-established direct access to God. Throughout the four Gospels, we read how Jesus states repeatedly that He had fulfilled prophecies, which all point back to the OT.

Then we also need to take into account all the eyewitnesses, the apostles and the people who believed in Jesus as well as the ones that defied Him. The Pharisees ended up having Jesus crucified by the Romans because they feared Him. They wanted to hang on to the old ways and remain in power over the church and the priests. They were afraid to lose their influence because Jesus represented a threat to them. The question here is why would anyone fear someone or something that didn't exist? Is this all a lie?

How can all the miracles of Jesus be explained? Not to mention other healings and miracles that took place long after the death of Jesus by His apostles. They are called the gifts of the Holy Spirit. How then is it is possible for anyone to speak a language unknown to them, exhibit unexplainable healing powers or have words of knowledge and prophesy at a drop of a hat? Above all, it is still occurring. Is this a lie too?

God's commandments may even be referred to as "The theory of eternal existence" or "The theory of a fulfilled and meaningful life". Or could we call it "The theory of perfection"? But every theory needs to be proven before it can be accepted.

In my humble opinion, there is enough proof. There is just too much physical and historical evidence to dismiss the existence of God. The chapter 'The Big Bang' brings it into perspective in a humorous way. Taking all this into consideration, can we still question the existence of God?

It doesn't matter how long you plow through these big questions, it is like the apple, no matter from where you start biting into it, you will always end up at the same core.

Which points right back to the core of the apple
.... *GOD WAS, IS AND ALWAYS WILL BE THE CORE*

*"...and God created everything, including the apple. He is the Alpha and Omega, the **Apple and the Core**."*

How did I find God?
- Back to the Beginning

Or should we say that it was God who found me? It has been a long and winding road with many wonderful experiences along the way and many more to look forward to.

Since I can remember, I believed in God. I grew up in a Catholic family. Both sides of my parent's families were of 'God fearing' people. This obviously meant that we had to go to church every Sunday. Does this sound familiar? In some ways, I was always drawn to the church. Years later, I became to realise what it was that I loved about the church. It was the actual building and the interior that gave me the sense of peace and security.

I was nine years old when my youngest brother was born and my father had then already passed away. When the time came for my baby brother's birth, dear friends of ours took my mum to hospital. My grandmother stayed with us kids and took us to church to pray. She walked us along the 12 Stations of the Cross and prayed with us. The prayers didn't make much sense but I kept looking at these 12 pictures and could not understand that no one had stepped in and rescued Jesus from so much suffering. Why didn't Jesus just walk away from it all to save Himself?

God did look after my mum and a healthy boy was born that day. I will never forget when suddenly the doors of the church were opened and someone called out to us: "It's a boy!" In the background, I could make out the soft glow of the evening sun as it was setting. It was one of my most unforgettable and treasured moments in my life, I was so happy.

Later on in my adult life, I only really wanted to step into a church when there was no service on. I'd just sit and look around at all the beautiful pictures and statues, thinking of all sacrifices these Saints would have had to endure and what extraordinary lives they had led.

I would look at Jesus on the cross and not even fully understand why He was crucified. All I really knew were some of the more well known stories of Jesus such as His birth, His miracles of healing, the wonders of walking on water, turning water into wine and of course His sufferings, death and resurrection. Many of us would have heard of these. Who actually understands the true meaning though? As for myself, I had no real concept of the true implications of the teachings of Jesus. Neither did I understand the significance of my First Communion at the age of nine. All that the First Communion meant was that, like the adults, I could go up to the priest and receive the Holy Communion. I became one of them, a grown up with the same 'privileges'.

Then came the day of my Confirmation. I was 13 years of age. All I understood was that we would receive the little flames over our heads. These flames are often shown as such on paintings with the apostles praying on the day of Pentecost. Our priest would have explained to us that the flames represented the Holy Spirit, but not in a manner that we could appreciate the meaning and enormity of this event.

On Alpha, the highlight of the course is to receive and be filled with the Holy Spirit (which are the 'little flames' above the head). We witnessed many amazing transformations. It is the most powerful encounter that one can experience. What a shame that the Confirmation doesn't take place at an age when one is mature and can recognise the significance of this amazing gift of Jesus.

Indeed, I did grow up as a Christian. However, what did I really understand? Every weekend we *had* to go to church. During the service, I could not wait to go home. I was so uncomfortable and intimidated by all these people around me. I felt that it was like a fashion parade, people watching one another, determining who is who and who has what. The service seemed so monotonous, a routine, going through the motions. All I could think of was what I was going to do after the service. In hindsight, a small seed must have still been planted on the inside but it took a long time to germinate and grow. Now here I am, sowing seeds and hope that they too will find fertile ground to grow in.

After each service I would visit my father's grave where I would pray and reflect. He had passed away when I was nine. The graveyard was situated further up the road from the church with a panoramic view of the lake and mountains. I would sweep my eyes across the scenery and talk to my father, imagining where my life would take me when I grew up. This to me was my church.

Many years later, I ventured into *New Age*. It was very fascinating to experience a variety of meditations and to explore the spiritual world. There, another chapter of my life had begun.

One of my hobbies is drawing. I always used to look out for new motives. One of the many ways I used to attain ideas and new inspirations was that a picture or an idea would flash through my mind in very vivid details. One evening I encountered one of those moments when an image of a man clothed in a hooded cape appeared before my inner eyes. I was so inspired by this unexpected vision and quickly grabbed my pencil to put it on paper. The man was facing my way, pushing open a huge double door. A bright light streamed through the open door behind him. I couldn't make out the details of the man as he stood in the shadow. When I started to draw, finer details slowly started to emerge. Initially I thought it was just an ordinary man dressed in a long cloak but as time went on, my pencil started to draw a big cross on his chest, just like the monks wear around their necks.

The cape appeared to be of noble appearance with impressive embroideries. I didn't pay any further notice of it, but intended to finish the picture one day as it made a terrific object. So I put the drawing aside and forgot all about it.

Three weeks later, I walked past a new age shop that had just opened. They were offering some free stuff, so I went in for bit of a browse. A man approached me and asked if I was interested to do a channeling course. This sparked great interest and I decided to partake in this course.

During the course, it turned out that the monk in my vision was in fact my spiritual guide. Later I realised that my vision foreshadowed many wondrous things to happen. It took me a long time to trust but after many proofs, I believed that he used to live in the medieval time. He kept saying that he was a protector of people. He would guide persecuted people through secret underground passageways into safety.

Many astonishing events occurred thereafter. It gave me a huge insight into what the spiritual realm is like. The most profound experience was during a meditation. I was channeling when all of sudden something out of the ordinary happened. With certainty, I knew that, at that very moment, I was connected directly to God. One cannot put such an amazing awareness into words.

For some strange reasons, my first reaction was that of guilt. I didn't feel I was worthy or significant enough to deserve any of God's holy and precious time. After all, who was I amongst the entire picture of Creation? How could my own smallness and insignificance even deserve the attention of God? Surely, there are others who deserve it much more than me. What have I done to qualify for the honour of a private audience with God!?

In this fleeting moment of total clarity, I knew that God is connected to every human being simultaneously. I even knew how this is possible. It all made perfect sense. Unfortunately, the how is no longer clear, but from that moment on, I knew God is alive and is with us all at the very same time.

Initially I hesitated to share this story; however, one cannot change one's own history. So, this is my 'crazy' story and it tells how God has prepared a path that ultimately led me back to Him. I intend be transparent and perhaps some of my readers can identify with my story and may even have had similar experiences. To draw our attention to Him, God can make use of many strange vehicles.

During the time whilst I was still involved in channeling, these words went through my mind whilst heading out in my car: *"We communicate through love, love is our telephone line to you."* This clearly signifies that we need to have love in our hearts towards God in order to 'hear' him. Therefore, pray with your heart, not with your head. Just be still for a moment and focus on your heart. Feel your love grow into a big flame in your heart.

The following verses from the Old and New Testament are referring to what I had experienced:

Whoever does not love does not know God, because **God is love***.*
1 John 4:8 (NIV)

But I am like an olive tree flourishing in the house of God; **I trust in God's unfailing love for ever and ever***.*
Psalm 52:8 (NIV)

If you want to progress on the right path in life (flourish like an olive tree, bearing good fruit), you need God's love. God has presented me with the gift of helping people as a physical therapist:

In order to increase my healing abilities, I had in mind that my spiritual guide could 'introduce' me to a spiritual healer. So, with my eyes closed I launched into a meditation. I was expecting that another human form would manifest. Instead, I was taken by surprise. A big bright light appeared and it said: "I am a great healer. I will be with you, but at the same time I'm in many other places with many other people." By now, you may start to see where this is all leading to: This light was Jesus. All along, I was led back to God and Jesus who had always been with me. Through His Holy Spirit, I was blessed to help others.

Now we are taking a quantum leap forward to September/October of 2010. Very special friends of mine had asked me to come to their church and I was very interested. I had just broken up from a relationship and was to move back into my house in December that year. It was a rather challenging time, but not traumatic. Still, I had questions and my self-esteem hovered a bit under zero.

On my first visit to the church, I took everything under scrutiny. Back then I was not even aware of who the Baptists were. I was even contemplating them being some sort of a sect. One can never be too careful. This church however, which has become my church, has taken me by storm. Everybody was so friendly and welcoming. After only a couple of visits, the pastors already acknowledged me. It is amazing what a welcoming *'how are you'* and a warm smile can do. Very quickly, I started to feel at home. What influenced me most were the sermons. They felt like they were customised to my own circumstances. During the days leading up to Sundays, I longed to find out what I will get to learn from the sermon. In as little as 5 weeks, I felt reaffirmed within myself. My confidence started to return. That was the turning point when I made a commitment to God. I prayed:

"Thank you Lord for helping me back on my feet and leading me to this wonderful church with such caring pastors and staff. The very least I can do to show my appreciation to you is to visit the church every Sunday."

This commitment is still standing and continues on. Compared to my childhood, I now look forward to going to church every Sunday. Apart from the worship and sermons, I found and made so many new friends. It feels wonderful to be greeted by name. As time went on, I put up my hand for a few volunteer positions at the church, which I enjoy. It is my way of contributing and helping others who are where I used to be.

At that time, my life started to change and go uphill rapidly. During a special church group function, I met a lovely lady. We connected and exchanged numbers. A few weeks later, I kept thinking about calling her to catch up. Then to my surprise, one Saturday afternoon the phone rang and it was her. She told me that she had a strong prompting from God to call me and asked me if I was interested to have a session with her. She is a psychologist as well as a Christian counselor. This sounded terrific, as I was at a crossroad, unsure of what I should be doing going forward. So, we met up at her place. We started off with prayers. With my permission, she called her friend who has the special gift of communicating with God. He was to ask God what message he could pass on for me on His behalf. I was very curious to know what he would come up with and anticipated something along the line of a future career change. He responded by asking me a question. God wanted to know what sort of relationship I had with my father. I was taken aback and almost started to laugh aloud. It was the farthest thing I had expected. Instead of talking about my future career move, he was asking me about my 'relationship with my father' who had passed away such a long time ago. This cannot be right; this can't possibly be God talking. Despite my doubts, I went along with it and it turned out to be exactly the right question. The first time in my life, I became to realise that all my insecurities and low self-beliefs were the shadow of my father's death.

We all deal with loss in different ways. Deep down in my subconscious mind I felt abandoned. I kept all my feelings to myself and would never share with anyone unless they asked me directly. My grief never really faded, it was only subdued by a busy life. I had led a life trying to find love, a special person that would love me for who I am, not for how I looked. I often felt very lonely despite having many friends. I was craving to find the right person to have a family with. That afternoon, I recognised that I had always based my ultimate happiness on finding the right person. Only by being with this person would I reach my ultimate fulfillment. I learned that all my life I was looking for love in the wrong places. I had never realised how close and accessible, in fact, love is. This was one of my biggest turning points in my life and loneliness became a thing of the past.

God is our Father and He loves us for who we are. I also became to realise that God has created me the way I am. I am perfect in His eyes. I don't have to do anything or be anyone specific to earn His love. His love is His free gift. All I need to do is to accept His love and love Him back to complete the circle. By turning the focus on my late father, God touched me at my most vulnerable point. Only later did it sink in that God was really there that afternoon. He was actually talking with me. Who else but Him could have known that this was a part of me that had never quite healed? With this simple question He released me from my pain and set me free to receive His love. He opened the door for me to finally step out as a free person and to know who I truly am. God told me that He truly loves me and no matter what, He is always there and nothing else will ever change this.

From this moment onwards, I scrutinised and criticised myself less and less. If I were to continue and find fault, wouldn't I then reproach God and His Creation? Everything He does is perfect and fits into His plans, including you and me. We all are convinced that there is always someone else or something better than us out there. A little voice inside us keeps whispering: *'I am too fat, too short, too tall, too ugly, too...etc.* Is anyone ever satisfied with what he or she has and how he or she looks? One can classify such discontentment as a direct insult to God. Imagine you were standing next to Michelangelo in the Sistine Chapel in Rome, looking at his picture of 'Creation'. Then you turn around and start telling this great master that the angels are ugly, Adam is out of proportion, the sky is too blue or the choice of colours is not right. In other words, you would be claiming that Michelangelo didn't have a clue about art. I wonder how this would come across to an artist who spent his entire life painting and sculpting?

God is the perfect maestro who designs each one of us in an unmatched uniqueness. How do you think He feels when people live in self-hate? By hating themselves, they hate God.

There is no need to worry what other people think of you. The only opinion I am now concerned with is that of God: Who I am, what I'm doing with my life and whether I utilise all my God given talents for my God given purpose. Am I implementing them appropriately in meaningful ways and areas? We humans are never happy with what we have and who we are. We constantly compare ourselves with others instead of counting our own blessings.

Each one should test their own actions. Then they can take pride in themselves alone, without comparing themselves to someone else,
Galatians 6:4 (NIV)

At the end of the session, my friend advised me to get rid of any figurines (idols) and disengage in any channeling activities with other spirits. A couple of times I had to swallow hard. At that time I couldn't understand why I wasn't allowed do this anymore. However, because everything that had happened during the session was so compelling that I agreed based on my trust I had in her. It wasn't easy, but I made a firm commitment. As I mentioned earlier, I was unsure if I could include my past channeling activities in the book as it clashes with the biblical and Christian doctrines. But this very season on my journey played an integral part in reconnecting with God.

Channeling, as well as other New Age practices, raises many questions for many new Christians. I felt that my transparency could assist some of you to understand why it ought not to be done. I too was grappling with this idea but, a few months ago, the rationale finally fell into place whilst writing this chapter.

When I started to read the Bible last year, I found quite a few verses where God warns us not to make contact with other spirits. The first few verses are from the Old Testament:

10 Let no one be found among you who sacrifices their son or daughter in the fire, who practices divination or sorcery, interprets omens, engages in witchcraft,

11 or casts spells, or who is a medium or spiritist or who consults the dead. 12Anyone who does these things is detestable to the Lord
Deuteronomy 18:10-12 (NIV)
Do not practice divination or seek omens.
Leviticus 19: second part of 26 (NIV)

31 Do not turn to mediums or seek out spiritists, for you will be defiled by them. I am the Lord your God.
Leviticus 19:31 (NIV)

6 'I will set my face against anyone who turns to mediums and spiritists to prostitute themselves by following them, and I will cut them off from their people.
Leviticus 20:6 (NIV)

19 When someone tells you to consult mediums and spiritists, who whisper and mutter, should not a people inquire of their God? Why consult the dead on behalf of the living? 20Consult God's instruction and the testimony of warning.
Isaiah 8:19-20 (NIV)

And in the New Testament Paul writes to Timothy:

1 The Spirit clearly says that in later times some will abandon the faith and follow deceiving spirits and things taught by demons.
2 Such teachings come through hypocritical liars, whose consciences have been seared as with a hot iron.
1 Timothy 1:1-2 (NIV)

At first, from a general perspective, one would not consider the communication with the spiritual world to be sinful nor described as 'bad'. One would wonder what could possibly go wrong by consulting a spirit. There is no harm done, right? Why then would God forbid us to do so in such a vehement manner?

It took me a long time to find the answer. But, one day, it all started to make perfect sense. I became to realise that if anyone was to channel, it had to be initiated and blessed by God Himself. For example, God's Spirit may not always communicate directly to us. Instead, He may appoint a 'courier' to pass on His message. We know them as angels of God. There are a multitude of such instances described in the Bible. I only picked a couple from the Old Testament:

2 There the angel of the LORD appeared to him in flames of fire from within a bush. Moses saw that though the bush was on fire it did not burn up.
Exodus 3:2 (NIV)

11 But the angel of the LORD called out to him from heaven, "Abraham! Abraham!"
"Here I am," he replied.
Genesis 22:11 (NIV)

and three from the New Testament:

The angel said to the women, "Do not be afraid, for I know that you are looking for Jesus, who was crucified.
Matthew 28:5 (NIV)

18 Zechariah asked the angel, "How can I be sure of this? I am an old man and my wife is well along in years."
19 The angel said to him, "I am Gabriel. I stand in the presence of God, and I have been sent to speak to you and to tell you this good news.
Luke 1:18-19 (NIV)

26 Now an angel of the Lord said to Philip, "Go south to the road—the desert road—that goes down from Jerusalem to Gaza.
Acts 8:26 (NIV)

We can also look at God's dominion the same way as the equivalent of a corporation or a business. There is a set hierarchy and chain of command in place, which has to be abided by. All decisions are made from the top and passed down. So by us talking to the dead and other spirits, using Ouija boards (aka witchy board), engaging in witchcraft and consulting mediums, we are 'bypassing' God, therefore breaking the law. God was, is and will always be the highest Being.

One needs to wonder what sort of information is being transferred from an *unauthorized* contact in the spiritual world. Considering all this, it is very harmful; a dangerous exercise that needs to be avoided at all cost.

I feel that God made contact with me through a spiritual entity of His own choosing. These experiences served their purpose but are no longer necessary. Now I 'channel' directly to God with my prayers, exactly as we are meant to. I still get answers and insights, but now I know that they are from God. Everything I have perceived since has always been 100% confirmed. It is an overwhelming feeling when God talks to you. No one talks like God.

Who else but God knows the absolute truth? In His perfect wisdom He knows what He can reveal and when. As we put our trust in God, there is absolutely no need to go anywhere else. Therefore the only way to know that the message is true is by talking directly to our Creator. Any so-called messages by any other sources from beyond cannot be verified nor trusted. In fact, it can be rather dangerous.

In the New Testament, the apostle John explains how we know that God is speaking with us:

1 Dear friends, do not believe every spirit, but test the spirits to see whether they are from God, because many false prophets have gone out into the world.
2 This is how you can recognize the Spirit of God: Every spirit that acknowledges that Jesus Christ has come in the flesh is from God,
3 but every spirit that does not acknowledge Jesus is not from God. This is the spirit of the antichrist, which you have heard

is coming and even now is already in the world.
1John 4:1-3 (NIV)

There are also other criteria that verify that the Spirit of God is speaking:

- Is it spoken in and with love?
- Does it line up with what the Bible teaches?
- Is it only for the good for self and others?

We need to be very mindful of how our actions and decisions will impact self and others. If you find yourself feeling compelled to do something that is only for personal gain or that it could hurt other people's feelings or end up harmful, definitely this is NOT God's voice.

Here is yet another way we can look at why we go to God directly. What do we do if we want to talk to our parents? Do we contact our neighbour or some friends first? Of course not, so it is with God. Why shouldn't we talk directly to Him? We do not have to be afraid of Him. He is God Almighty, but not too almighty that He wouldn't respond to His children.

"You shall not make for yourself an image in the form of anything in heaven above or on the Earth beneath or in the waters below.
Deuteronomy 5:8 (NIV)

Sometimes we need to stop a certain activity, even if we can't understand why at the given time. With trust and faith the answers will come. When you commit to God, you let go of anything else that does not belong. The same happens when you get married; you don't hang on to your ex-boyfriends or girlfriends. Nor do you let your eyes wonder in search for someone else because you made a vow to your spouse, in love.

*37 Jesus replied: "**Love the Lord your God with all your
heart and with all your soul and with all your mind.'***
Matthew 22:37 (NIV)*

I had made a decision to follow Jesus and channeling
was one of the things that no longer lined up. Who else do I
need when I have Jesus in my life? Who else could possibly
be stronger and possess greater wisdom? My heart has found
a safe home and I haven't felt lonely ever since. It allows me
to be happy and positive. Of course there are times when I am
out of kilter, but it never lasts long, because I know whom I
can turn to for help and encouragement. Often, when I
contemplate the serious state our world is in, I'm so grateful
that we have Jesus. Who else have we got?

*Which points right back to the core of the
apple…God, who is our eternal refuge*

God's Creation - the Human

'May the LORD bless you from Zion,
he who is the Maker of heaven and Earth.'

Psalm 134:3 (NIV)

Before God formed His first human, he created a planet called Earth that is capable of sustaining life amongst the suns, moons and all the other planets. Imagine we were to look up in the night sky and would only see the moon? How odd would that be?

On Earth God masterminded all that we need for our existence and to enjoy its beauty and perfection, the heavens and Earth, day and night, the seasons, forests and deserts, oceans and rivers, vegetation and animals. This was the order of His Creation. Then He segregated us from all there is and made us ruler of the Earth, because we are God's precious crown jewels.

26 Then God said, "Let us make mankind in our image, in our likeness, so that they <u>may rule over the fish in the sea and the birds in the sky, over the livestock and all the wild animals, and over all the creatures that move along the ground</u>."
Genesis 1:26 (NIV)

He has entrusted us with complete freedom and authority. As 'rulers', we are created with the capacity and intelligence to evolve, develop and advance in technology.

However, we do not possess the wisdom that can reach beyond this world and therefore we rely on our Creator. Unfortunately, many people do not realise that the universe does not revolve around them, but it is the human who revolves around the Source of all life, God. God is our Heavenly Father and looks after His children as we do as parents for our children. We set 'rules' for our children for the very same reason that God has given His laws to us. Like our children, we are not mature enough to know yet. God's guidelines are guardrails to keep us safe and to lead us back to Him.

God has specific plans and we all play a part in it. Our existence is not an accident. God does not just amuse Himself with us when He happens to get bored. A befitting example is to conceive humankind as very valuable and irreplaceable paintings or sculptures in an art museum. They have surpassed many hundreds of years because the curator (God) has diligently kept the environment in optimal condition. At times, restoration work would be conducted to maintain the integrity. Until now, and for generations to come, they have been on display to give delight. Such artifacts are not created to be locked up somewhere in a dark storage room. No artist would invest his time and brilliance to create something that is so exquisite and precious without a purpose, nor would God. With our incredible abilities, we truly are the crown of Creation and stand out like "a town built on a hill".

"You are the light of the world. A town built on a hill cannot be hidden.
Matthew 5:14 (NIV)

I like the passage in which Jesus refers to us as being the salt of the Earth. I have read this passage several times previously, but was never quite able to comprehend its meaning. Not so long ago I was studying the Gospel of Matthew with my lifegroup. I knew that this passage would inevitably come up. I had no idea how to explain it when the question was going to be raised. I did what we all need to do; I trusted and asked God to give me clarity. The answer did present itself on that night:

Evidently, Jesus knew that salt is one of the most important and necessary minerals on this planet. Its merits are indisputable, so are ours. For this reason He has chosen this analogy. We have been created for a purpose. Unlike animals, we are set apart. The reason for our existence is to evolve and perfect ourselves. Animals on the other hand have only a basic purpose. They are here to serve us as livestock or as companions to enjoy. Naturally, we no longer need them as much for work as we used to in the past due to advanced technology. In third world countries, elephants, horses, mules and oxen are still very much needed for their great strength and endurance.

These verses point out that humans cannot just 'bathe' ourselves in God's Glory and aimlessly drift through life. We are all born with specific God given talents to fulfill our God given purpose. Each of us has responsibilities to self and others. If we don't take action we lose our saltiness, we become useless. Jesus tells us that we are the light of this world and ought to help others to do so too.

The Bible tells us that we are children of God, created in His image. Many people like to think that God looks like us as we are created in His image.

So God created mankind in his own image,
in the image of God he created them;
male and female he created them.
Genesis 1:27 (NIV)

In reality it refers to the spiritual body, not the physical body. Our souls carry the 'same DNA' as God's. The body is not eternal, but the soul is. Therefore it is impossible to even fathom a likeness to the physical appearance of our Creator.

Clearly, God has created our souls from His own Being. He then has given it a body to be able to experience and sustain a physical life to grow, learn enjoy and not to suffer. The body has been fashioned in such perfection that the anatomy leaves scientists still stupefied. The entire maze of our DNA strands, chromosomes and cells functions in absolute harmony.

Have you ever speculated over the Creation of humans? Every single human being, since 'Adam and Eve', has always been completely individual and unique. There never has been another you somewhere else, nor have there been any 'double-ups' or 'repeat specimens'. Who can possibly accomplish such feat and still continue to come up with brand new Creations?

The blueprint of a human is too intricate for a person to comprehend, unless you studied anatomy or physiology. Let's just compare the *God Made* Human and the *human made* robot. Ever since time began, the greatest aspiration of human kind, beside the ability to fly, was and still is to create a life form, a human that is immortal. So far, they have come up with some outstanding machines, computers and robots. The robot is mechanical and has programs and commands that can be adjusted and modified. Could it be that they are getting close? But there is a 'slight' difference between the *God made Human* and the *human made robot,* an imperative component. God has given us the breath of life and has 'implanted a microchip' called soul. This microchip runs one programme that cannot be overwritten: our free will as well as the ability to distinguish between good and bad.

Our soul contains a *folder*, which is labeled '*God Space*'. It cannot be deleted or modified (access denied): a subconscious desire to search for our Creator and fill the empty space, to give us the peace and fulfillment we so yearn for. I am absolutely convinced that humans will never be able to create a living being. We are not capable to produce the *breath of life*. The soul is definitely the final frontier. There are limits to how far we can go as mere mortals. Without God there is no life. He is connected to all. Humans, animals and plants can only sustain as long as God breathes life into it.

Without God, no seed would ever germinate nor any child born take the first breath. Neither would any animal, on land, in the air and in the water take in the breath of life. We may be the rulers of this Earth but we need to remind ourselves that it is only by the Grace of God. With it come the responsibilities of a leader. As leaders we are accountable for our actions and therefore need to adhere to certain rules and act on the consent of the ONE who owns it all. However, many people are convinced that there is no such thing as a soul.

Since I can remember, I have always thought that we have a soul. As a child I used to ask myself, assuming that there is no soul, why would it hurt so much in the chest when someone very close dies? Why would we feel joy and happiness in our heart? Is it the heart as an organ that feels or is it the soul? Is an organ capable of experiencing pain and joy created by circumstances and emotions?

To my limited understanding and according to my logical conclusion, the physical heart really has no reason to be affected by any emotional occurrences; therefore it won't feel pain. The purpose of the heart is purely mechanical; it supplies the body with blood by pumping it through the veins. Emotional pain is not caused by a chemical reaction. Quite the opposite, our emotions elicit chemical reactions such as adrenaline, which affects our body to react.

In light of this, is it the heart or is it the soul that feels the pain, hurt, sorrow, anger, hate, love, joy or happiness? It can only be but the soul. I have always resorted to this explanation when conversations were around this topic. To my understanding that in it self proves the existence of the soul. As always, we can find the answer in the Holy Bible:

7 Then the LORD God formed a man from the dust of the ground and breathed into his nostrils the breath of life, and the man became a living being.
Genesis 2:7 (NIV)

Our souls need God to survive. Without this connection we can never be a complete being, no matter what we have accomplished. People continue searching for that special something and when they get it, the emptiness within continues on. Little do they realise that in actual fact, it is God they are craving for. If the 'God space' remains empty, so does life. When we have 'found' God, we know that we have arrived home; we have *fully-filled* our 'God Space folder'.

Another way of looking at the existence of the soul is the example of a car. A car (human body) is fully functional. It won't work without the driver (consciousness/intelligence). But in order to start up the engine, the driver needs a key - God, who gives the breath of life.

There is an inconceivable amount of untapped potential in all of us. We are designed and capable of so much more, which links in with chapter 'God given Talents and Gifts'. Most of our abilities appear to be 'de-activated' as we do not trust and believe in ourselves, having lost the connection to the SOURCE. To either retain or re-activate our programme, in either case we need to be connected to the mainframe computer - God. He has provided us with the necessary time to upgrade and maintain our systems (nurture our souls); outlined in the Fourth Commandment:

8 "Remember the Sabbath day by keeping it holy.
9 Six days you shall labor and do all your work,
10 but the seventh day is a sabbath to the LORD your God. On it you shall not do any work,
Genesis 20:8-10 (NIV)

11 For in six days the Lord made the heavens and the Earth, the sea, and all that is in them, but he rested on the seventh day. Therefore the LORD blessed the Sabbath day and made it holy.
Genesis 20:11 (NIV)

13 For you created my inmost being;
you knit me together in my mother's womb.
14 I praise you because I am fearfully and wonderfully made; your works are wonderful,
I know that full well.
Psalm 139:13-14 (NIV)

Which points right back to the core of the apple…God, our Creator

The BIG BANG
- Genesis Chapter 1, Verse 1?

"In the beginning there was nothing,
..........and then there was the BIG BANG."

(someone's version 1:1)

How would this version of Genesis sound? Was there a Big Bang? Was this the beginning? Now, here is a trivial question for people out there who are true followers of the "Big Bang" theory: If we were to assume that it did happen, *WHO then would have pushed the button*?

For a moment, let us just go along with the Big Bang theory. Let's say that there was a big explosion somewhere once upon a very, very long time ago. We are not going to worry about what could have triggered off such an event, let's say it just happened by itself.

From that explosion, planets, moons, suns, solar systems and galaxies started to pop up; aligned in perfect order. Then some billions of eons pass. Whenever the time was right, after a few more billions of years, some plants started to sprout up here and there. Maybe it took some more millions of years for animals to appear on this planet, perhaps on other planets too? Some more millions of years later, there was man; born in its perfection, just like that. Then, what an evolution, the human decided to get up and walk around. It would have appeared to be much easier that way. Now evolution had started to set its course, creating millions of different life forms on land, in the water and in the air. All occurred by itself, how amazing! The diversity and magnitude is mind-boggling.

To this day scientists are still trying to figure out how it all came to be. No clear answers as yet, not to my limited knowledge anyway. As a matter of fact, they haven't been able to reach any conclusions. Quite the opposite, they are getting more and more overwhelmed by the ingenious and complex configuration of basic life. So what happens when one cannot come up with any solid scientific evidence? One may begin to look at other possibilities. What else can there be and who has all the answers? I guess it would have to be the Creator himself.

There are a number of scientists who, after many years of research have come to their final conclusion that the beginning of Creation couldn't have happen by accident. They could not find a valid and satisfactory explanation to the biggest mystery, the Creation of life. Nor could they account for the complex programming of a simple cell or the composition and design of the DNA. Had there been just one minuscule mistake in a critical piece of the DNA, there would not be life. It can only be the work of a supernatural entity. As a result, some of the scientists felt compelled to turn towards God and ended up as fervent Christians.

Now, let us go back to my first question to who pushed the button. I cannot fathom the idea that an explosion can happen without being triggered off by someone or something. Nothing can come out of nothing, $0x0=0$ or $0x2=0$.

As I was drafting this chapter, the first scientist that came to mind was of course Stephen Hawking. He is the most famous and brilliant mind of today and we can be so grateful of what he has been able to discover. As he also stated, there was nothing before, no time and space. I came across this quotation on the Daily Mail News website:

"The Big Bang didn't need God to set it off", says Stephen Hawking;
19.04.2013 Daily Mail News

There are so many different viewpoints, which make it to such an interesting and much disputed topic. Personally I find it impossible to get my head around the idea that out of a total void came the biggest bang there ever was. Having said that, I am not a theoretical physicist, a cosmologist or scientist. This is only my own personal opinion, not a fact. I'm just trying to open up the minds of the readers to a different perspective, sprinkled with bit of humour. I hope you are having a bit of a chuckle too.

In the midst of all this, there is also the evolution theory to consider. Enough physical evidence has been collected by archeological discoveries over the years to give us a picture as how this planet evolved. All sorts of life forms, crustaceans, plants and animals that have been extinguished for millions of years, in-bedded in what was once soil and now solid rock, have been found all over the world. Yes, planet Earth has evolved and still evolves, nothing remains the same. There is life and there is death. The cycle never stops.

We are still assuming that there was a big bang; here is another question that I cannot find a logical answer to: What could have possibly set the start of evolution in motion? Someone had to be there to write a 'programme' initially. The best analogy I can come up with is that of a computer without any software installed. How is it feasible to operate the computer without software? One can't possibly write a programme without having any software installed in the first place. Hence the computer cannot 'evolve' to the capacity of processing data and perform complex functions. What happens when the hardware, e.g. the big bang, is switched on? The lights would come on, like the explosion, but then what? There is nothing to work with and we would only be staring a blank screen. So who created the software? Who wrote the blue print and who designed absolute perfect harmony in nature, the so-called food chain? You would have all watched National Geographic's, David Attenborough or any other wildlife documentaries at some stage. Next time you do, just for a moment, imagine that all these amazing creatures happen to be just a so-called fluke. Yes, that would include you too. Are we all just accidents? Is this really it?

That takes us back to the very start:

"In the beginning there was nothing...?"

Can one really create something out of nothing? Zero multiplied by any figure will always equal zero. Or perhaps was there a red button? 'Someone' or 'something 'must have initiated a type of action for it to happen. Our whole existence must have evolved out of something. There had to be a plan, a design, a function, anything that allowed humans, fauna, flora and planet Earth to develop to its present state. Is there a Creator? Maybe we do find the answer in the Bible on page one after all; it reads like this:

> *"1 In the beginning God created the heavens and the Earth.*
> *2 Now the Earth was formless and empty, darkness was over the surface of the deep, and the Spirit of God was hovering over the waters."*
> *Genesis 1:1-2 (NIV)*

It starts with "*In the beginning GOD...* So there was "something" or "someone" there before the beginning.

Or taken from the New Testament (the apostle John refers to Jesus as the "Word"):

> *1 In the beginning was the Word, and the Word was with God, and the Word was God.*
> *2 He was with God in the beginning.*
> *3 Through him all things were made; without him nothing was made that has been made.*
> *4 In him was life, and that life was the light of all mankind.*
> *John 1:1-4 (NIV)*

> *5 But they deliberately forget that long ago by God's word the heavens came into being and the Earth was formed out of water and by water.*
> *2 Peter 3:5 (NIV)*

Who created the human being? Was it God or evolution?

A really funny scenario pops to mind. If it was just random evolution, imagine in another few millions of years from now, dogs could start to talk back at us? Dolphins (who have a very developed brain) would mutate and grow legs and arms and get out of the water and walk straight to the government houses and start ruling the world? What if all the animals that had their fill of being mistreated, shot and hunted down as a sport, would grab some guns to defend themselves? Would this also be classified as another freak of nature? Perhaps the Big Bang theory supporters may want to watch out?

When we take a look at us today, we humans have such powerful brains to develop and further ourselves, to continuously expand our horizons, experience life and to understand the meaning of our existence. What all the pioneers, explorers, philosophers, scientists, artists etc., since ancient history have achieved is amazing.

'The current state of our planet Earth, human development, technology, science and inventions is the summation of the entire human existence since Creation."
~ Monica

This raises even more questions. How far can we delve into unknown territories in the pursuit of immortal life, proof of the afterlife, Creation and God? Are there any set limits as to how far we can go? Are there boundaries in how much more we can exploit humans, animals and other life forms by altering the DNA or other types of experimentations? How far are we really allowed to go?

This verse came to mind:

15 The Lord God took the man and put him in the Garden of
Eden to work it and take care of it.
16 And the Lord God commanded the man, "You are free to
eat from any tree in the garden;
17 but you must not eat from the tree of the knowledge of
good and evil, for when you eat from it you will certainly die."
Gen 1:15-17 (NIV)

Could it be that the *'tree of knowledge'* also represents the parameters that God has set for us? Is this the "Keep Out" sign for humans? We can never get to know everything nor would we be capable of comprehending the magnitude of the whole truth in this lifetime. God only reveals as much knowledge as He sees appropriate for each individual. Even if God were to reveal every detail of Creation to us, we wouldn't have the physical capacity to understand. We live in a different dimension to God's, therefore different laws apply. It would be like trying to explain to a blind person what a rainbow looks like. A person who was born blind would not even understand the concept of colour. Nor would a person who was born deaf understand the concept of a melody. How could a deaf person possibly imagine the sound of a piano when he has never heard any sound at all?

Really, we only need to know that it was God who created everything that exists, an uncreated Mastermind who *is* before the beginning. And is it so important? What would change if we were to get a glimpse behind the curtain? Would it satisfy our curiosity or destroy what we have in the here and now? Could this 'glimpse' cause a 'replay' on what happened in the Garden of Eden?

Now may be the time to reconsider and invest our earthly time into things that truly matter. When looking at our planet Earth, isn't it amazing how everything is provided to sustain all life forms. Every plant that produces fruit or vegetables covers the entire spectrum of nutrients that are needed to live a perfectly healthy life. Every animal, on air, land or water, exists in a perfect cycle of survival, an ongoing food chain. In the meantime though, humans have modified plants and animals by adding chemicals, changing DNA and altering cells structures. Now there are some things that are no longer in their original state; therefore unable to produce the nutrients that they were originally designed to yield. The intelligent species, classified as *Homo Sapiens*, have overwritten a perfect programme to allegedly better and improve the performance of agriculture and farming. We have been handed over an environment that balances to perfection across fauna and flora. However, in our own wisdom, we are trying to reinvent the wheel and meddle with matters that should best not be touched. Instead of centering our attention on spiritual growth, we throw our efforts into things that are meant to be off limits. How is it possible to perfect something that already is perfect? By taking into account the entire perfection of Creation, I personally believe that this would nullify the Big Bang Theory; life cannot just be an accident.

God has given us the responsibility and control over all creatures and this Earth; not to change or destroy it, rather to rule with respect and love; in a manner of keeping it intact and safe. God has set us up comfortably so that we can spend our time with Him. Sadly, the majority of the human race misses the point; they are searching for physical evidence rather than investing their precious life in the pursuit of spiritual growth. The ultimate outcome ought to be that our desire is to reconnect with God and live together in peace as a big family.

Shipwrecked:

Picture yourself shipwrecked in the middle of the ocean. You are lost and trying to keep afloat. You are scared that no one would find you. Then, in the far distance, you notice the biggest and most amazing luxury cruiser you have ever seen. You are so relieved and refreshed with hope to be rescued. What are you going to focus on? Would you stop swimming, trying to find out where the cruiser came from? Are you desperately trying to work out what the cabins look like or what sort of room service you will delight in? Maybe you wonder with how many courses the grand dinner is served and whether you will be sitting at the captain's table? Isn't life like this? Instead of paying attention to the current situation, we throw ourselves into all sorts of irrelevant speculations that won't take us to our final destination, this absolutely stunning luxury cruiser.

Adrift in the water, wouldn't you rather swim as hard as you can and give it your very best to get closer to the cruiser so that they can spot you? You would find ways to swim faster and at the same time preserve your energy. You may even splash the water around you to get noticed and be saved. Do we 'splash around' in life when we want to be saved? God will not intervene if you just drift around, preoccupied with worldly dreams of great wealth, fame or power. You must give it your very best to progress and learn so that God will notice you and help you along. You don't even have to splash around you. As long as you swim towards God, He will, beyond any doubt, send out a rescue boat and throw a life jacket to pull you on board. At that moment you are saved. You have arrived at your desired destination and will even get to sit at the captain's table.

These days many may agree that science and religion are not on opposite sides, rather, they go hand in hand. Unlike hundreds of years ago, religion suppressed science, scared that they could lose control over people. Some religions were based on fear to stay in power. In those days, working class people, who were the majority, couldn't afford education and therefore were easy to manipulate. Fortunately, things have had a huge turn around and religions since have realised the science is not a threat; on the contrary, it proves the existence of a Creator - God.

Which points right back to the core of the apple…God, the Maker of all

Does God heal?

Does God really heal? This is another big question that most people are asking. Some are hoping and praying for healing, some don't believe that there is even a God who heals.

To this day, we still find actual evidence of miraculous healing. People who are told that there is no hope have been known to recover from their terminal illness. A cancer may clearly be evident on a scan and on the next follow up it doesn't show any more. It leaves doctors baffled because there is no logical explanation. When I hear about these kinds of recoveries, the love and immense power of God overwhelm me.

Being a physical therapist part time, this is one of my favourite topics and very close to my heart. I love reading the passages in which Jesus is healing the sick with absolute fascination.

> *...So he (Jesus) said to the paralysed man, "Get up, take your mat and go home."*
> *Matthew 9:6 (NIV)*

It would have been so amazing to witness how a person, who, for a lifetime had never been able to walk, all of a sudden gets up and walks. The legs would not have had any muscle tone and too weak to carry the weight. But, they still got up, *'took the mat and went home'*. Apart from the cause of the paralysis, the muscles would have also had to be restored to perfect condition.

Perhaps there is another way we can describe a 'healing by God'. What if we were to call it: reinstating the perfection of His Creation?

That takes me back about two years, (yes, whilst driving my car...) when an unexpected question popped up in my mind. What exactly happens when God heals? How does He do it? How can it even take place? It was like looking at a picture, trying to work out what it is that the artist wants to express. My conception about healing took a completely new outlook.

I sensed that I was led to the conclusion that Jesus didn't actually heal people. This only expressed an outward picture. But when we view it with our heart and spirit, it takes on a completely different image: **Healing is the result of an action, not the action itself**. So what IS the action? In chapter "*Who is God*" you will find the answer. The verse of 1John 4:8 plainly points it out: **God is love**. God is the pure and everlasting force of love. Love is the most powerful energy, therefore capable of anything. Nothing can ever overrule love nor can anything be stronger than love. So, when *touched* by God, how then could evil possibly exist?

We will hold this thought for now before going to the 'action'. Let's go back to the beginning. Why and how can it all go wrong in the first place? Illnesses and disabilities can be the result of a variety of reasons. Of course not all can be explained and remain unanswered. I have listed four categories that can outline some of the possibilities:

1. An impure existence

Such is inevitably influenced and controlled by evil. Allow me to expand on this a bit further as it may sound rather preposterous at first glance. Living a life of sin is also called living a life outside God's parameters/laws. It just does not work. Therefore, being oblivious of the connection between body, mind and spirit, one unwittingly allows it to happen.

These days, people are convinced that they either have no time or there is no necessity for reflection and spiritual growth. Instead, they bypass God or even worse, convince themselves that there is no God and evil. They are preoccupied and stuck within the materialistic world. There is more about this in chapter "*What do I pack for my Journey Home*". Just as King Solomon exclaims in Ecclesiastes: ...*is meaningless, a chasing after the wind*. We are 'starving' our soul of 'spiritual nutrients'. As a result, the body and/or mind can eventually be affected by 'chasing' after the wrong things and begin to deteriorate in health.

As part of the curriculum for the Life Coaching Certificate, we had to write a research project. I was inspired to outline the fact that, any kind of issues that we are facing that are not dealt with, in the end, will manifest in the body somehow. Next to my own experiences with clients, I have also referenced with other authors, therapists and doctors. If you would like to find out more, you can visit following link to the summary version:

http://mmrlifecoaching.com/MMR_Life_Coaching/Mind_over_Body.html

Published to the general public and being conscious of other beliefs, I haven't put God into the equation directly. Who else but our Creator can fill the gap? There really is no option whether or not there is a need to engage ourselves with our spiritual counterpart. Quite the contrary, it is an absolute necessity. If we don't, we slip away and get lost. There will always be this emptiness in spite of what we have acquired and achieved. It can result in any of the following: dependency to addictive substances or activities, depression, loneliness, mercilessness, anger, guilt, low self esteem, jealousy, immoralities, cruelty, revenge or crime. Eventually, the body will suffer the consequences.

As the saying goes: which is better, to live poor and happy or rich and unhappy? Which doesn't mean that one has to be poor to be healthy and happy. Not in the least, it all depends how we balance our focus on accumulating wealth and investing our time and resources. Does the world evolve around you or do you live in it? Do you contribute to society? Are you watching out for others?

1 Jesus stepped into a boat, crossed over and came to his own town.
2 Some men brought to him a paralysed man, lying on a mat. When Jesus saw their faith, he said to the man, "Take heart, son; your sins are forgiven."
3 At this, some of the teachers of the law said to themselves,

In these verses Jesus truly demonstrates that our spirit is of greatest importance. He didn't just get this man back on his feet. First Jesus forgave his sins and healed his soul. He gave him a fresh start. By this alone, the man would have been happy because he was set free and given hope by Jesus. This is what it means when we say that Jesus is our saviour. The spirit needs to be restored before the body can be cured.

2. Lesson to be learned

Another reason could be that the person is meant to learn a particular lesson. It could also be that God is opening a door to get her of him back on the right path. People like this may have become totally lost and overcome by darkness. God knows that this is the only kind of 'wake up call' that will work. It is not a punishment; it is indeed a blessing from God. Such people would surely impact others around them and become a free spirit just as the man did who had encountered Jesus.

3. Become God's instrument

Many people who face significant health challenges appear to demonstrate great inner strength. Despite their suffering, they are happy and filled with inner peace. Is God speaking through them? Are they conveying to us what really counts?

I was trying to find the story that I heard of a boy that got almost all of his body burned. Unfortunately, I couldn't find it but I came across one of many burn survivor support websites that I didn't even know existed. Reading their stories of courage and strength made me feel so grateful not to have had to go through such ordeals and to appreciate my health and wellbeing.

Could these people be some of many of God's instruments? Are they teaching us that we are capable of much more than we can imagine? Each one of these people on this site would have impacted a large circle of family, friends as well as the doctors, therapist and readers.

I do hope these stories and testimonials are being read by many more. It teaches us to count our blessings and to stop looking at the 'bad' stuff in our lives. Instead, we ought to appreciate what we have and what we can share with others.

Not being sure about the legalities, I didn't feel I could copy the story of a man in America whose body is scarred by two-thirds. He had overcome his insecurities and now embraces the scars as part of him. Another example is the incredible story of **Nick Vujicic.**

(These are extracts from "The Blaze" - 5th June 2014 http://www.theblaze.com/stories/2014/06/05/born-with-no-arms-or-legs-he-tried-to-end-his-life-at-age-10-now-hes-inspiring-millions/):

"For many years I felt it was sort of foolish to believe that God loved me when he gave me less than everyone else,"
"I was in bed and I realized, 'I either can be angry for what I don't have or thankful for what I do have,'" he said. Two years later, at age 15, Vujicic became a Christian and eventually came to believe that God really did have a plan for him. All of his uncertainty began to wash away. Vujicic said he soon began allowing God to use his personal pain to help others. He had his first speaking engagement at 19.

There are countless stories that are so amazing and awe-inspiring. It is very humbling to learn of such people's lives and it prompts us to take stock of our own circumstances. Maybe we are doing just fine.

4. A propellant to greatness

No one wants to suffer or be disabled just to achieve significant accomplishments that serve for the good of humankind. But an illness or disability can become a blessing in disguise and bring forth phenomenal greatness and exceptional strength. To turn a disadvantage to an advantage takes great courage and determination. God can do amazing things and work in unexpected ways. It may be that it can give a person that certain kind of 'fuel' to forge forward and produce such outstanding accomplishments. I can only list a few famous people that fit into this category, but there are many more such talents in the world with incredible courage of whom we may never get to hear of.

Beethoven: *Continued to compose music from when he started to turn deaf at the age of 26, during that time he contemplated suicide but decided to live on and continue with his art; something that requires immense dedication and vision. To this day we are thankful that he pursued his genius. Imagine a world without his symphonies…*

Stephen Hawking: *One of the most famous physicists in the world, who was diagnosed with ALS (form of Motor Neurone Disease) at the age of 21. He holds 12 honorary degrees. Hawking poured himself into his work and research, convinced that he might not have much longer to live. His work has significantly affected the exploration of General Relativity and Quantum Gravity. It has propelled scientific research forward in a great way and gives others the advantage to build on his findings.*

Stevie Wonder: *Has greatly influenced the world of music and composed many songs that will continue to live on. He was born premature which resulted in a growth defect in his eyes. Had he not lost his eyesight, would he have ever discovered this wonderful gift and pursued music? Due to his blindness, his body compensated by enhancing the hearing abilities above the norm and hence, may have given him the* *extra edge.*

President Franklin Delano Roosevelt: *Led America through the difficult times of WW2. He succumbed to Polio at the age of 39. He was in office 1933-1945. I believe that his example gave hope to many others suffering from Polio, which was much more common than in this day and age. His outstanding courage inspired the American people never to give up, just as he didn't during the tough times of WW2.*

Frida Kahlo: *From Mexico, contracted polio at the age of 6 and became a world famous artist painter, most known for her self-portraits. Her illness didn't stop her from being herself and contribute to art.*

Helen Keller: *Was the first deaf-blind person to earn a university degree* (Bachelor of Arts), *she was an author and an activist for women's and labour rights with considerable influence.*

Lenin Moreno: *Was shot at by robbers that left him paralysed at 45, after 4 years of agonising therapy he later became involved in politics, was vice president of Ecuador and made a huge impact on the needs of disabled people in his country. He was nominated for Nobel Prize 2012. All this he accomplished from his wheelchair.*

These remarkable people could have just given up. What would the world look like today? How many people's lives have been touched and changed by what they are and have endured? Would they have become what they are if they had not been stricken by health challenges? We will never find out but we know that they never gave up and set an example of determination and tremendous courage. I am positive that God played His part in healing their spirit and transforming them to such greatness.

When talking of healing, we tend to focus the attention only on the physical aspect, expecting God to restore the body back to perfect health. When this does not occur, we get disappointed and think that God hasn't 'lived up' to our expectations.

We tend to ignore the importance of the spiritual health. What we may not be aware of is that God may have in fact healed a person's heart whilst the physical ailments remained. The person is still 'trapped' in a compromised body, however, the spirit is set free, with new hope; inspired and refreshed to recognise the true purpose of life.

The human spirit can endure in sickness, but a crushed spirit who can bear?
Proverbs 18:14 (NIV)

We also need to be aware that not all people want to get healed. They either decide consciously or it happens subconsciously without them being aware of what is going on in the spiritual stratum. God can only heal, if a person asks and truly believes. The soul, which is a part of God, is then in agreement. If God would just go ahead and heal the sick out of His love and compassion, He would be in breech of His very own law; He would go against our free will. God has given us a free will, the freedom to decide for ourselves. In summary, it would go against our own will/agreement because we have not asked for healing. Somehow it all fits into a greater plan that we have no way of comprehending.

Another reason that prayers may not get answered is that we pray for the wrong things. In many circumstances we ought to perhaps pray for healing of the mind and ask God to help us overcome and deal with old wounds that still hurt deep inside, traumas or other unresolved personal issues. As mentioned above, the mental state can have a physical effect and begin to manifest in the body in form of pain, a disease or an illness. By healing the mind and spirit, the body is given a chance to follow suit. There are many such examples.

I hope by pointing out some of the possibilities that could trigger off a disease and what they could represent, we can start to see that God does heal. Of course there is still so much that we cannot find answers to.

Now lets get back to our thought of what the action of healing represents. Roughly two years ago a sudden thought entered my mind and I became to realise the fact that Jesus healed by 'transmitting' the energy of love. Luke, who by the way used to be a doctor, describes the exchange of energy in the following verses.

45 *"Who touched me?" Jesus asked. When they all denied it, Peter said, "Master, the people are crowding and pressing against you."*
46 *But Jesus said, "Someone touched me; I know that power has gone out from me."*
Luke 8:45-46 (NIV)

In other words, Jesus 'zapped' the body with a force so powerful that it totally eradicated all imperfections and impurities, anything that does not belong. This energy is called LOVE. The body is reinstated to what it was before it got 'polluted'. So the **action *is the touch of God's Love***. I am convinced that the energy of pure love is capable of totally obliterating anything that is not from God. It replaces all imperfections with the Creator's perfection. Evil, in this case sickness, cannot exist in the presence of love. The light of love does not leave any shadows for evil to hide in. In a synagogue, a man with a crippled hand approached Jesus to ask for healing:

He (Jesus) looked around at them all, and then said to the man, "Stretch out your hand." He did so, and his hand was completely restored
Luke 6:10 (NIV)

Is it a miracle or is it the wonder of God's Grace?

There are so many stories told about miracles that Jesus performed throughout his ministry. He was most famous for his death and resurrection, but His miracles have left us all in awe of His endless power. Many of the healing occurred also in conjunction with driving out demons (healing of the mind).

Action and result come as a package deal. It doesn't just involve physical healing but the spirit too has to be restored. It is all connected and represents our whole existence. For instance there cannot be only a hand, it connects to a forearm - upper arm - shoulder - collarbone - neck - scull - brain and last but not least, the spirit.

And how does God get into action? What makes Him decide to help you? The first and foremost important step is faith. Lack of faith hinders us from receiving the true love of God. Here is how the verses continue from where Jesus felt His power going out of him:

47 Then the woman, seeing that she could not go unnoticed, came trembling and fell at his feet. In the presence of all the people, she told why she had touched him and how she had been instantly healed.
48 Then he said to her, "Daughter, your faith has healed you. Go in peace."
Luke 8:47-48 (NIV)

These verses clearly point out what is needed: In **FAITH** she touched Jesus. By doing so she **ASKED** for healing, therefore she was **HEALED** by Jesus, with her 'permission'.

To recap the meaning of healing:

Healing is the outcome; LOVE is the action.

"I truly believe that, if God was to touch us with His 'undiluted' love,
we would simply disintegrate.
His perfect and pure love is too intense for us to withstand in its unmatchable purity.
When touched by God, how then can evil exist?"
Monica

Which points right back to the core of the apple…God, our Healer

Does God still care?

Many people these days are questioning if God still cares. Has He abandoned us? Why is there so much turmoil on our planet? Everywhere we look we can see little sparks that are on the brink of erupting into an inferno; wars, crime and natural disaster have become a daily occurrence. Some of us ask why does God allow this to happen?

Here is one way to look at it, but as mentioned again later on, these are not all the answers but it may open up a brand new way of understanding this complex topic a bit better.

As tough as it may sound, in my opinion, the misery on this planet is self-inflicted. God didn't start wars, neither does He commit crimes, we do. When we encounter hardships we pray and ask God for help and when nothing happens we get frustrated or angry like little kids. Unfortunately, this is not how it works. God is not a Fix-It-All institution.

We have allowed our perfect planet to be devastated with pollution by the abuse of natural resources. We have allowed the extinction of precious animals and plant life and we are still ignoring all the warning signs. There is no point to pop a tablet to make ourselves feel better, nor will false prayers get us out of our predicament. The root of such devastation and hopelessness lies within us. So why do people blame God for their misfortunes? It certainly was not a part of God's plan. There is no hope in the absence of God. The Old Testament gives us the best examples of how many times God rescued and delivered His people from their misery and oppression, despite them turning away from Him over and over again.

Everything was created with love and perfection. We have been entrusted with a perfect and flawless planet. The way we have and still treat our environment and people around us has thrown it out of balance. Our shortsightedness and greed has led us astray. We are heading straight towards self-destruction. For some, this may sound like fiction, but it all points to our free will, which is a great gift and privilege entrusted to us by God. As it turns out, it is our biggest and hardest challenge to yet overcome.

Naturally 'free' people are inclined to choose their own path. It takes an exceptional character to be able to stick the ego in the back pocket, trust, learn and follow instructions, considering that the source is invisible - God.

The Bible is filled with stories of such men and women who put aside their own wants and needs and made room for what God intended for them to do. They put their full trust and life completely into God's hands.

The reality is that being willing to 'choose to be willing' means that we apply our free will. To hold God's Will above ours is the only way we can put a stop to all evil. Then love can rule the world where there will be no breeding ground left for evil to fester. If we are not willing, then we also have to take on the responsibility for the outcome and wear the consequences.

There never is a bad day for a good deed. Every day and every second presents itself as a new beginning. It is never too late to start afresh. Every day God reaches out and gives us countless opportunities to reconnect with Him and reconsider our current direction in life and to change. The Bible calls it 'repent'. In order for our situation to change, WE are the ones that must change. Can we? Can you? God knows, ask Him.

Which points right back to the core of the apple…God, who never gives up on us

Why Does God punish us?

This is a question that we all ask ourselves at one point in time. Why would a loving and gentle God punish us? Isn't He supposed to look after us and love us? Why does He treat some of us so harshly? At times, it may even appear that there are people that just don't get a break. Yes, we are yet again taking another bite from our mysterious apple to get us closer to the core.

11 My son, do not despise the LORD's discipline,
and do not resent his rebuke,
12 because the Lord disciplines those he loves,
as a father the son he delights in.
Proverbs 3:11-12 (NIV)

Know then in your heart that as a man disciplines his son, so
the LORD your God disciplines you.
Deuteronomy 8:5 (NIV)

During one of my Bible readings, I found the answer to my question. These verses stood out as if they were highlighted. I sensed that God wanted me to stop right there and add a new chapter with the thoughts that came through. It explains it so clearly why criminals, murderers, thieves, egocentrics, corrupt and merciless people seem to get away with 'murder'.

People who live outside the law often live a life that lacks of nothing; all appears to go so well for them. They prosper and make a lot of money, live in big houses and drive expensive cars. They don't have to work like the majority of us. They can jet around the globe without a care in the world.

How can this be? Is this fair? One really wants to ask God on what side His justice lies. Don't we all ask ourselves the same questions? Why are the 'good guys' doing it so tough and the 'bad guys' have it all? Why don't they get punished instead of us? Why do so many righteous people live in poverty? Wouldn't they deserve to live a comfortable life? After all, they are good upright citizens or Christians, helping other people, never afflict any harm onto others or break the law. Millions of disadvantaged people on this planet don't even have sufficient food or shelter. They live as social outcasts in the streets and in ghettos, struggling just to survive another day.

It just doesn't add up. The Old and New Testament talk so much about God's mercy, His love for *all* mankind. Why doesn't He look after the needy ones and people who live by His laws? Doesn't that leave the impression that God 'rewards' bad deeds and 'punishes' the good?

Let's have another look at the verses. Could it also read that the word suffering stands for learning and shaping one's character? Could this be the approach that God uses to teach us just as our parents do? After all, He is our Heavenly Father. When we were kids we could never understand why we weren't allowed to do certain things. Our parents punished us or told us off when we misbehaved. Was it really so bad when we came home late or didn't tidy up our room? When we grow older, the pieces start to fall into place, especially when we get to have our own kids. Mostly we tend to follow in our parent's footsteps. As a typical teenager I couldn't always see eye to eye with my mother. I am sure many of you can identify with my story or have experienced similar battles:

Like any growing teenager, I had a boyfriend. We used to go out Saturday nights. My mum was adamant that I was home by 12:00 am. I was then allowed to spend time with my boyfriend at home.

It didn't make any sense to me why I had to be home 'so early' on a Saturday night?! I felt my mother was so way out and old fashioned. In my opinion then I concluded that she just didn't grasp how the world went around those days and hadn't caught up to the current times yet. My mum's point of view was that any decent girl is not to 'lurk around' in the streets after midnight. I tried to make her understand that we didn't do anything 'naughty'. We were just hanging out in the discos (Now you can guess my age...).

I justified that we had to leave the disco at the latest at 11:30pm to make it home in time. This was exactly the time when it got busy and the real excitement started.

Eventually she gave in a bit and allowed me to be home by 12:30-1:00am. This was a little win, but still not good enough for me, but at least I was able to squeeze in some extra time.

When I grew older and thought back, I actually admired my mother for giving me such freedom. I even thought that if I had had a daughter, I would have locked her up, out of harm's way. The thought of all the possible dangers out there would have petrified me. My way of thinking has certainly shifted since. But back then, how many times did we have quarrels, how many times did I feel misunderstood and how often did I feel that my mum overreacted and didn't love me.

Many years later, I started to realise how privileged I was to have had such wonderful, loving and ethical parents. I was very lucky that I had a mother who only wanted the very best for me. She protected me from ruining a good future for my life by starting out on the wrong path.

Without a moral upbringing, where would I be today? Who would I have turned out to be instead? In the end, I believe I turned out to be an ok person with the right fundamental principles. My 'sufferings' were well worth it…

Parents who don't love and care for their children enough let them get away with anything and allow them too much freedom. They are just too busy and tired, worrying about work and paying the bills in time. It is much easier and requires less effort to say yes than no. Putting down the foot and making the children stick to the rules can be very overwhelming and draining. It results in arguments for which there is not always enough energy left to deal with. To make up for their own shortcomings, they spoil their children even further with gifts and allowances. This can often happen in families who live on higher incomes. These kids take advantage of their 'freedom' and try anything that they know is bad for them. The school bags are tossed in a corner and they hang out with their mates, contributing nothing towards their future. Who cares anyway, there is plenty of money around. These poor kids are lacking guidance and feel lost and tend to consider themselves an unwanted burden. Subconsciously they yearn for a strong and confident leadership within the family structure. Their misbehaviour is in fact a cry for help and a means of drawing attention. It is the only way they know how act. Unfortunately they often don't get heard. Good examples of these kids are the ones of famous or very wealthy parents. Many of them end up with drug addictions that often lead to suicide. Unaware of the consequences, they destroy themselves with drugs and alcohol in the hope that it would drown the pain and loneliness.

The not so 'privileged' kids feel like their parents hate them. They are not given all these expensive toys, holidays, the latest gadgets or even sporting opportunities that their rich peers have. They perceive their parents as mean and are oblivious of their predicament. Children are incapable of seeing the bigger picture. They learn from their parents and follow their example.

Let's have another look at Proverbs 3 verse 12:

"because the LORD disciplines those he loves, as a father the son he delights in."

I believe this sentence answers the question. This was the punch line that stood out for me. The Trinity of God: God the Father, Son and Holy Spirit. God is our Father; he has created us with tenderness and love. The human being is His treasured possession, His crown jewel. How then could He not love us? We are His children.

So, who do we classify as 'good parents'? Are these the

parents that spoil their kids and let them have anything they desire or the ones that teach them discipline, morals and ethics? Is it comfortable and easy to discipline children or does it sound like fun? Not at all, but for the best possible future it's worth every tough confrontation, anguish and heartbreak endured in the process.

As adults, we are just like children. We are continuously growing, exploring new territories to widen our perspective. We have all heard it before; you never stop learning. The moment you do, you die. So it is with 'feeding' our soul with what it needs, the Creator.

Jesus answered, "It is written: 'Man shall not live on bread alone, but on every word that comes from the mouth of God.' "
Matthew 4:4 (NIV)

We need to learn how to love and trust Him, the same way as we trust our earthly parents. No father would ever give second best to his children, nor does God. As kids we listen to our parents. We depend on them and even more so, we love them. We respect and trust their judgment and follow their instructions. If children don't love and respect their parents, they won't be obedient and will choose their own way. So it is with us grownups. If we want to respect God's sovereignty, trust His decisions and follow His ways, we must first love Him as our Father and God. Then we will start to listen and act accordingly.

In the Gospel of Matthew, Jesus tells us:

9 "Which of you, if your son asks for bread, will give him a stone?
10 Or if he asks for a fish, will give him a snake?
11 If you, then, though you are evil, know how to give good gifts to your children, how much more will your Father in heaven give good gifts to those who ask him!
Matthew 7:9-11 (NIV)

We ought to live our life with this in the forefront of our

mind. It is difficult for us to trust; especially when it concerns someone we cannot physically see. It takes time, but the sooner we do so the more we can take advantage of what God has in store for us. Trust means to let go of control and hand it over to our Creator. Maybe this is the reason why the word **trust** is a word that gets repeated so often in the OT and NT (*trust* appears 96 times in NIV; a total of 142 times in different tenses).

We cannot believe unless we trust and cannot trust without belief. You can go to Chapter 'Why Faith' which talks specifically about faith and trust. What precedes trust and belief though is LOVE. It all hinges on love.

To follow God's purpose is not always a walk in the park. It requires a lot of love and trust as well as discipline, which often is associated with struggles and disappointments. There is nothing worth more than putting your trust in God. The reward is a lifetime of inner peace, joy, purpose and love and ends with the promise of eternal life. We are only here for a very short time compared to eternity. What is more important, the here and now or what is waiting for us in eternity?

Such is when discipline is required during which our trust and faith is being tested:

- Events that don't go according to expectations
- Disabilities
- Disadvantages
- Loss
- Pain
- Disappointments
- Conflict
- Abuse & hurt

When we overcome these temporary 'discomforts', we will always come out on the other side as winners, strengthened in faith and grateful for the experience to learn and grow.

Allow your Father in Heaven to guide and discipline you.

Permit Him to love you and continue to work on and within you. Take these tests and trials in a stride. Thank Him for loving you enough to care and teach you.

> *(Jesus) Those whom I love I rebuke and discipline. So be*
> *earnest and repent.*
> *Revelation 3:19 (NIV)*

This is the second part of the equation: **those He loves!** As I was reflecting over this verse, it all began to make sense. It changed my perception of the so-called 'injustice'. The same applies to us. Parents who love their children raise them with a firm hand. They apply discipline to get them on the right track. Kids learn and make mistakes. No parent would throw their arms up in despair and give up on them. Mistakes are essential in order to grow and learn. They will be patient with their children, stand by them and continue to guide, teach and look after them.

However, there are children who will not comply and insist on being ignorant, no matter how deeply their parents love them and whatever they do for them. In total disregard they decide to take the easy road. They grab whatever comes their way. Their parents will eventually have to give up and allow them to go their own way and find out for themselves.

Is there a difference when we apply this to God? Could it be that God too has left those, who do not listen to Him, alone? Is this why they don't get disciplined and punished? Is this why it appears that they lack of nothing? They display immense wealth, fame and good fortune. Do they really? We can only see it from the outside. What will, one day, happen to them in eternity?

Here is the question again which we asked earlier on at the beginning of the chapter:

7 Why do the wicked live on,
growing old and increasing in power?
8 They see their children established around them,
their offspring before their eyes.
9 Their homes are safe and free from fear;
the rod of God is not on them.
Job 21:7-9 (NIV)

And it concludes:

22 But God drags away the mighty by his power;
though they become established, they have no assurance
of life.
23 He may let them rest in a feeling of security,
but his eyes are on their ways.
24 For a little while they are exalted, and then they are gone;
they are brought low and gathered up like all others;
they are cut off like heads of grain.
Job 24:22.24 (NIV)

On the contrary, nothing gets unnoticed, both the good as well as the bad. In the end, it will all come to its merited close. It is rather disturbing to even fathom that God would stop disciplining anyone. That He would turn away His face; what a terrible thought.

Think again; is it really worth following the easy road when being tempted? It only looks easy but once on it, the thorns will soon appear and the feet will get weary. Where does this road lead to and where does it end? There is no one there to watch over us. We surely have been 'left alone'.

In the Gospel of John, 15:1-2 (NIV) Jesus proclaims:

1 "I am the true vine, and my Father is the gardener.
2 He cuts off every branch in me that bears no fruit, while
every branch that does bear fruit he prunes so that it will be
even more fruitful.

He refers to us as His branches, God the Father is the gardener who only prunes the ones that want to grow and bear fruit. The others will be cut off and burned.

The ax is already at the root of the trees, and every tree that does not produce good fruit will be cut down and thrown into the fire.
Matthew 3:10 (NIV)

Do you really want God to stop 'pruning' you and leave you alone? Every physical body has an expiry date, but NOT the soul. The soul belongs to God, provided that it wishes to follow its Maker.

Whoever turns away from God and follows the evil ways will ultimately end up in the darkness.

God is infinite, the great "I AM" and we too are everlasting. The question is what road is your soul going to be travelling on? Is it the path that is lit up with God's love and grace or is it the pathway to oblivion. Who is it that you would have waiting for you at the Pearly Gates?

In these verses 'she' refers to wisdom:

13 Blessed are those who find wisdom,
those who gain understanding,
14 for she is more profitable than silver
and yields better returns than gold.
15 She is more precious than rubies;
nothing you desire can compare with her.
16 Long life is in her right hand;
in her left hand are riches and honour.
17 Her ways are pleasant ways,
and all her paths are peace.
18 She is a tree of life to those who take hold of her;
those who hold her fast will be blessed.
Proverbs 3:13-18 (NIV)

This kind of wisdom is what we will receive when we consistently and with absolute trust follow God's ways. The wisdom here refers to God's laws and universal principles.

And he said to the human race,
"The fear of the LORD—that is wisdom,
and to shun evil is understanding."
Job 28:28 (NIV)

Why 'Us against God', our Father? Why is it that so many people either turn away from God or just don't want to hear about it? Most of us have, at some stage, heard of the Ten Commandments written by God on stone tablets. Chapter *'Why not sin'* will cover the commandments in details with examples and explanations that relate to us today.

If we then were to consider and understand what God's Commandments represent, could we understand God's intentions and plans for us? Would we still consider Him as being bossy by putting us under His thumb and 'punishing' us? Or would we understand that He is acting as the loving Heavenly Father whose only intention is for all of us to flourish?

Can you picture a world where every single person follows God? It is that of a perfect world:

- No crime
- No sickness
- No poverty
- No wars
- No jealousy
- No hunger
- No hatred
- No favouritism
- No cruelty

Such is a world that He desires for all of us. He longs to equip us so that we can succeed in life and have the best of everything possible. Do we want to be pruned or do we want to be cut off? Do we want to take up the challenge or do we really want to be left alone?

I never realised that there are so many references to the reasons of God's discipline until now. When things are being repeated so many times we must conclude that it is important. These verses summarise what we have learned and underline the significance of it:

5 And have you completely forgotten this word of encouragement that addresses you as a father addresses his son? It says,
"My son, do not make light of the LORD's discipline,
and do not lose heart when he rebukes you,
6 because the LORD disciplines the one he loves,
and he chastens everyone he accepts as his son."
7 Endure hardship as discipline; God is treating you as his children. For what children are not disciplined by their father? 8 If you are not disciplined—and everyone undergoes discipline—then you are not legitimate, not true sons and daughters at all.
Hebrews 12:5-8 (NIV)

Which points right back to the core of the apple…God, who is our loving Father

My prayer:

*My Father in heaven, thank you for loving and
caring for me.
Thank you for waiting for me to respond and accept
you in my life. Thank you for being patient and to
teach and discipline me.
Thank you for correcting my mistakes and not
giving up on me.
Thank you for not turning away from me despite all
my wrongdoings.
I am so grateful for all the lessons I have learned
and will still learn that prepare me for my
homecoming.
I pray that you wait for me with joyous anticipation.*

Amen

Why Jesus?

Who is Jesus?

15 "But what about you?" he asked. "Who do you say I am?"
16 Simon Peter answered, "You are the Messiah, the Son of the living God."
17 Jesus replied, "Blessed are you, Simon son of Jonah, for this was not revealed to you by flesh and blood, but by my Father in heaven.

Matthew 16:15-16 (NIV)

Many people still don't believe that Jesus really is the Messiah. Some are still waiting for Him and others either don't believe in a Messiah or don't even know about Him. Perhaps you are in doubt yourself? You may have asked this very question so many times before. How can we be so sure that Jesus really is the Son of God? Even at Alpha, this is the first topic that is being discussed.

It is claimed that there are in actual fact over 300 prophesies in the Old Testament that foretell the birth of Christ with exact details of His life, death and resurrection. The Old Testament was written by so many different authors between 1400 to 450 years prior to the birth of Jesus. Comparing the counterparts of the OT and NT, it is literally impossible NOT to believe that Jesus was and is the Messiah, the Son of God and part of the Trinity of God.

The beginning of the Gospel of John (NT) starts with proclaiming who Jesus really is:

*1 In the beginning was the **Word,** and the **Word** was with God, and the **Word was God**.*
*2 **He was with God** in the beginning.*
*3 **Through him** all things were made; without him nothing was made that has been made.*
4 In him was life, and that life was the light of all mankind.
John 1:1-4 (NIV)

It is also very interesting to notice that in Genesis (the first book of the OT), chapter 1 verses 1 to 25 God refers to Himself as first person singular. Then in verse 26 He uses first person plural, **US**. Despite having read these passages on numerous occasions, I kept overlooking the meaning. I was so surprised when I recognised the connection of these verses. This is an example of the mystery of the Bible; it only reveals what you need to know. Obviously I was only focusing on the actual Creation and totally missed the finer details.

*26 Then God said, "Let **us** make mankind in **our** image, …*
Genesis 1:26 part of (NIV)

God uses first person plural in this verse, indicating that He is not One, Jesus is there with Him.

In Genesis chapter 1, second verse, God first introduces the third part of the Trinity, the Holy Spirit.

*And the Earth was without form, and void; and darkness was upon the face of the deep. And **the Spirit of God moved** upon the face of the waters.*
Genesis 1:2 (NIV)

God the Father, the Son and the Holy Spirit

Now let's turn our attention back to the prophecies. How were they actually fulfilled by Jesus? These events have all been documented in the New Testament by eyewitnesses who were there at the time when it happened and were in physical contact with Jesus.

In the left column of the table below are the prophesies from the OT. On the right hand side, you will find the fulfillments. I have only selected some of the most commonly known events. We can find many other references to Jesus in the Psalms and by the Prophet Isaiah.

(All verses quoted are from the **N**ew **I**nternational **V**ersion (**NIV**))

The birthplace: The prophet Micah predicts Bethlehem to be the birthplace and Nathan in 2 Samuel tells King David of Jesus. The Gospel of Matthew starts with the genealogy from King David to Jesus.

Old Testament	New Testament
"But you, Bethlehem Ephrathah, though you are small among the clans of Judah, *out of you will come for me* *one who will be ruler over Israel,* *whose origins are from of old,* *from ancient times."* *Micah 5:2* ———————— *12 When your days are over and you rest with your ancestors, I will raise up your offspring to succeed you, your own flesh and blood, and I will establish his kingdom.* *13 He is the one who will build a house for my Name, and I will establish the throne of his kingdom forever.* *14 I will be his father, and he will be my son.* *2 Samuel 7:12-14*	*So Joseph also went up from the town of Nazareth in Galilee to Judea, to Bethlehem the town of David, because he belonged to the house and line of David* *Luke 2:4* Spoken by an angle to the three shepherds: *Today in the town of David a Saviour has been born to you; he is the Messiah, the Lord.* *Luke 2:11*

The virgin mother Mary, you can also find it in Luke 1:31	
Old Testament	New Testament
Therefore the Lord himself will give you a sign: The virgin will conceive and give birth to a son, and will call him Immanuel. *Isaiah 7:14*	*This is how the birth of Jesus the Messiah came about: His mother Mary was pledged to be married to Joseph, but before they came together, she was found to be pregnant through the Holy Spirit.* *Matthew 1:18*

John the Baptist	
Old Testament	New Testament
A voice of one calling: *"In the wilderness prepare the way for the Lord ;* *make straight in the desert a highway for our God.* *Isaiah 40:3*	*John replied in the words of Isaiah the prophet, "I am the voice of one calling in the wilderness, 'Make straight the way for the Lord.'* *John 1:23*
"I will send my messenger, who will prepare the way before me. Then suddenly the Lord you are seeking will come to his temple; the messenger of the covenant, whom you desire, will come," says the LORD Almighty. *Malachi 1:1*	*And he will go on before the Lord* *Luke 1:17*

Jesus performed **numerous miracles** some of which include healing, feeding thousand with a handful of bread loafs and fish, raising the dead, banishing demonic and evil spirits, commanding the wind, walking on water, money or a great catch of fish; but most of all is His own resurrection and ascension. His first was turning water into wine.

Old Testament	New Testament
5 Then will the eyes of the blind be opened and the ears of the deaf unstopped. 6 Then will the lame leap like a deer, and the mute tongue shout for joy. Isaiah 35:5-6	Then they brought him a demon-possessed man who was blind and mute, and Jesus healed him, so that he could both talk and see. Matthew 12:22 42 Jesus said to him, "Receive your sight; your faith has healed you." 43 Immediately he received his sight and followed Jesus, praising God. Luke 18:42-43 But I (Jesus) want you to know that the Son of Man has authority on Earth to forgive sins." So he said to the paralysed man, "Get up, take your mat and go home." Matthew 9:6

Jesus the saviour, the word saviour appears 24 times in the New Testament

Old Testament	New Testament
Say to those with fearful hearts, "Be strong, do not fear; your God will come, he will come with vengeance; with divine retribution he will come to save you." Isaiah 35:4 The stone (Jesus) the builders rejected has become the cornerstone; Psalm 118:22	and you will receive a rich welcome into the eternal kingdom of our LORD and Savior Jesus Christ. 2 Peter 1:11 They said to the woman, "We no longer believe just because of what you said; now we have heard for ourselves, and we know that this man really is the Savior of the world." John 4:42 "From this man's (King David) descendants God has brought to Israel the Savior Jesus, as he promised. Acts 13:23

Palm Sunday Jesus rode into Jerusalem on a donkey, proclaiming that He is the Messiah	
Old Testament	New Testament
Rejoice greatly, Daughter Zion! Shout, Daughter Jerusalem! See, your king comes to you, righteous and victorious, lowly and riding on a donkey, on a colt, the foal of a donkey. *Zechariah 9:9*	*30 "Go to the village ahead of you, and as you enter it, you will find a colt tied there, which no one has ever ridden. Untie it and bring it here. 31 If anyone asks you, 'Why are you untying it?' say, 'The LORD needs it.' " 32 Those who were sent ahead went and found it just as he had told them.* *Luke 19:30-32*

Jesus mocked by the people	
Old Testament	New Testament
6 But I am a worm and not a man, scorned by everyone, despised by the people. *7 All who see me mock me; they hurl insults, shaking their heads.* *8 "He trusts in the LORD," they say, "let the LORD rescue him. Let him deliver him, Since he delights in him."* *Psalm 22:6-8*	*39 Those who passed by hurled insults at him, shaking their heads 40 and saying, "You who are going to destroy the temple and build it in three days, save yourself! Come down from the cross, if you are the Son of God!" 41 In the same way the chief priests, the teachers of the law and the elders mocked him.* *Matthew 27:39-41* *He trusts in God. Let God rescue him now if he wants him, for he said, 'I am the Son of God.'* *Matthew 27:43*

Crucifixion, Jesus was nailed on the cross	
Old Testament	New Testament
16 Dogs surround me, a pack of villains encircles me; they pierce my hands and my feet. 17 All my bones are on display; People stare and gloat over me. 18 They divide my clothes among them and cast lots for my garment. Psalm 22:16-18	23 When the soldiers crucified Jesus, they took his clothes, dividing them into four shares, one for each of them, with the undergarment remaining. This garment was seamless, woven in one piece from top to bottom. 24"Let's not tear it," they said to one another. "Let's decide by lot who will get it." This happened that the scripture might be fulfilled that said, "They divided my clothes among them and cast lots for my garment." So this is what the soldiers did. John 19:23-24
"And I will pour out on the house of David and the inhabitants of Jerusalem a spirit of grace and supplication. They will look on me, the one they have pierced, and they will mourn for him as one mourns for an only child, and grieve bitterly for him as one grieves for a firstborn son. Zechariah 12:10	Instead, one of the soldiers pierced Jesus' side with a spear, bringing a sudden flow of blood and water John 19:34

24 And they crucified him. Dividing up his clothes, they cast lots to see what each would get. 25 It was nine in the morning when they crucified him Mark 15:24-25 |
| My God, my God, why have you forsaken me? Why are you so far from saving me, so far from my cries of anguish? Psalm 22:1 | About three in the afternoon Jesus cried out in a loud voice, "Eli, Eli, lemasabachthani?" (which means "My God, my God, why have you forsaken me?"). Matthew 27:46 |

No bone to be broken

Old Testament	New Testament
19 The righteous person may have many troubles, but the LORD delivers him from them all; 20 he protects all his bones, not one of them will be broken. Psalm 34.19-20	But when they came to Jesus and found that he was already dead, they did not break his legs. John 19.33 These things happened so that the scripture would be fulfilled: "Not one of his bones will be broken," John 19:36

No decay, Resurrection

Old Testament	New Testament
10 because you will not abandon me to the realm of the dead, nor will you let your faithful one see decay. 11 You make known to me the path of life; you will fill me with joy in your presence, with eternal pleasures at your right hand. Psalm 16:10-11	29 "Fellow Israelites, I can tell you confidently that the patriarch David died and was buried, and his tomb is here to this day. 30 But he was a prophet and knew that God had promised him on oath that he would place one of his descendants on his throne. 31 Seeing what was to come, he spoke of the resurrection of the Messiah, that he was not abandoned to the realm of the dead, nor did his body see decay. 32 God has raised this Jesus to life, and we are all witnesses of it. 33 Exalted to the right hand of God, he has received from the Father the promised Holy Spirit and has poured out what you now see and hear. Acts 2:29-33

Jesus ascended	
Old Testament	New Testament
When you ascended on high, you took many captives; you received gifts from people, Psalm 68:18	*8 This is why it says: "When he ascended on high, he took many captives and gave gifts to his people." 9 (What does "he ascended" mean except that he also descended to the lower, Earthly regions ? 10 He who descended is the very one who ascended higher than all the heavens, in order to fill the whole universe.) Ephesians 4:8-10* *After he said this, he was taken up before their very eyes, and a cloud hid him from their sight. Acts 1:9*

For some of you all this may come as a surprise just as it did for me. I never knew that the coming of Jesus was prophesied; not to mention that Jesus had fulfilled over 300 prophesies. When I was going through the BiOY (Bible in One Year) programme in 2014, reading the OT left me absolutely stunned. Some of the events of and around Jesus were described in such details that, speaking of myself, it left me with no doubts that Jesus is the Son of God.

Surely, no one would have read the OT back then and replicated what the prophets were writing just so that they could claim to be the Son of God. Imagine, being fully aware of what is going to happen and knowing that they would have to endure the most gruelling death?

Just suppose you are having the Last Supper with your closest circle of friends and telling them that one of them is going to betray you? I would have run away, but not the Son of God. Even this was prophesied along with how much money Judas received and what happened with it.

12 I told them, "If you think it best, give me my pay; but if not, keep it." So they paid me thirty pieces of silver.
13 And the LORD said to me, "Throw it to the potter"—the handsome price at which they valued me! So I took the thirty pieces of silver and threw them to the potter at the house of the Lord.
Zechariah 11:12-13 (NIV) OT

Which points right back to the core of the apple…God, who loves us so much that He sent His only Son to save us

The Stargate JC

Jesus answered, "I am the way and the truth and the life. No one comes to the Father except through me.

John 14:6 (NIV)

Jesus is our Gateway to God, to our home and final destination. Whilst I was contemplating how I could best portray this image, the Science Fiction TV series called "Stargate SG" came to mind. Perhaps some of you may remember it. When they wanted to travel into space they had to make use of the Stargate to get there. First they had to have the correct coordinates to their destination. Once they punched in the numbers, the Stargate would engage. The frame of the gate started to turn around until it reached the right setting. A liquid looking wall then appeared which meant that the Stargate was open to either receive or to send people through. The crew then jumped through this liquid wall without seeing beyond it. After only a few seconds of travelling through something that looked like a space wormhole, they landed on another planet, light years away. They never really knew whether they would get to the right place and what was waiting for them, but they still walked through. I used to love watching it, wishing that this were possible in the real world. Little did I know that we actually can.

If we were to apply a bit of our imagination, we would realise that Jesus is our Stargate. The easy part is that the coordinates to our destinations are already programmed by God. We don't have to try to find them first.

I (Jesus) am the gate; whoever enters through me will be saved.
John 10:9 (NIV)

Jesus either receives or sends to and from God. Compared to the TV series, the 'Stargate JC' (**J**esus **C**hrist) is absolutely safe. We know that there is no danger awaiting us when we come out on the other side of the wormhole. Neither do we have to be scared of what we will receive through the 'gate' from Jesus.

All we need is to take a leap of faith and step through the "Stargate JC". We don't know on what planet, meaning our life, we are being taken to, but we can be absolutely certain that God has equipped us with all the tools we need to live on this 'planet' that is our life. We can also be assured that it will be exactly the right planet that each one of us has been assigned to until we reach our final destination.

Wherever Jesus takes us in life, we just need to follow Him; He guides us with His Spirit and by His infinite wisdom, sending it to us through His Stargate. Jesus has made it possible for us to communicate directly to God, which was no longer possible since Adam and Eve ate the forbidden fruit from the tree of knowledge.

15 The LORD God took the man and put him in the Garden of Eden to work it and take care of it.
16 And the LORD God commanded the man, "You are free to eat from any tree in the garden;
17 but you must not eat from the tree of the knowledge of good and evil, for when you eat from it you will certainly die."
Genesis 2:15-17 (NIV)

Prior to that, God would walk around in the garden with Adam and Eve, having conversations with them. They were naked because there was no shame; they were still 'pure'. After they were tempted by the serpent (devil) and ate from the tree of knowledge of good and evil, they hid from God out of shame. This was the first sin and it separated us from God. If we remain separated, we *will certainly die.* By that, God tells us, unless we change, our soul is unable to return and adapt to His dimension. It would surely perish.

God has created us in His image, which is pure love, but our pure souls were tarnished by the 'first sin'. The Bible describes it metaphorically, but it would have been such an earth shattering and devastating event that changed the course of history for humankind. It was an event so indescribable that God turned His face away and proclaimed humans as sinners.

An impure soul cannot exist in the collective of the universal vibration, which we call love. Love is the only thing that ultimately connects us all to God in His spiritual domain. Chapter 'Why no Sin' will talk into more detail of what sin is.

To this day, we still get drawn to actions and reactions that defy God's laws. But it doesn't have to be this way. Many people have been able to resist and recognise that the only way to find the absolute salvation and a sure ticket to paradise is to follow Jesus and the Word of God. They have stepped through the Stargate JC and never looked back. We all are given the same opportunity. God will not reject anyone whom Jesus sends, no matter of their past. He has never stopped loving us.

Throughout the Old Testament we can see how God demonstrated His love for humankind. He gave instructions through His prophets and He presented us with the Ten Commandments on the stone tablets. But it deemed to be not enough, so He sent His Son to reconcile us with Him. Through the death of Jesus we were made right with God again.

For God so loved the world that He gave His only begotten Son, that whoever believes in Him should not perish but have everlasting life.
John 3:16 (NIV)

I believe that there are three distinct dimensions, life here on this Earth, God's dimension and the dark side, the evil dimension. They run parallel. Whilst we live on Earth we need to make our own choices. What we will choose now will ultimately either take us back into God's dimension or to the other, that of darkness. We can only exist in one or the other, but not both.

Life here on Earth is tangible; we can see, touch, breathe, hear and feel. God's dimension is spiritual, invisible to us. The same applies for the evil side. Physical life has an expiry date; God's dimension is endless. God's dimension is real; life on Earth only lasts for a fleeting moment and it's over in a blink of an eye.

It is not what we acquire but it's all about the essence of what we aspire. Through His only Son, God has given us a way back to His dimension, our Stargate JC. Are you ready to jump through?

Which points right back to the core of the apple…Jesus, the Son of God who ensures eternal life for our spirit

Did Jesus die for US?

When Jesus died on the cross, not only did the day turn into night, but also the rocks split and the Earth shook. It would have had to be an extremely frightening moment for the people in Jerusalem, the doomsday before the end of the world. In a sense it was. The death of Jesus was the death of the old ways and the birth of a new life of hope. Above all, the curtain in the temple tore in half:

50 And when Jesus had cried out again in a loud voice, he gave up his spirit. 51 At that moment the curtain of the temple was torn in two from top to bottom. The Earth shook, the rocks split
Matthew 27:20-51 (NIV)

Note: also recorded in the Gospel of Mark (15:38) and Luke (23:45).

The tearing of the curtain played a very significant part in what the death of Jesus represented. This curtain used to separate the people from the Most Holy Place in the temple where God dwelt. Only the High Priest was allowed to go beyond this point on the Day of Atonement, which was held only once a year. The curtain is also referred to as *the veil*. It measured 28 cubits long and 4 cubits wide (1 cubit=51.9cm). This would make it over 14 meters high and 2 meters wide according to my calculations.

With His death, Jesus removed all the barriers that stood between God and us. The moment Jesus died; the curtain tore apart, exposing the Most Holy Place to all the people. Now we all have access 'beyond the curtain'.

On the day of the 'first sin' in the Garden of Eden, the Stargate got shut down. Jesus had come to re-activate the gate for us and will let anyone through who believes in him. We are all equal, no one has to pay an entry fee nor can it be earned in any way. It is a free gift from God. The sacrifice of

Jesus has gained direct access to God for us. Just as Adam and Eve were in the beginning, we now can have a personal relationship with God.

This is what Jesus promises us when we acknowledge and accept Him in our life:

28 "Come to me, all you who are weary and burdened, and I will give you rest.
29 Take my yoke upon you and learn from me, for I am gentle and humble in heart, and you will find rest for your souls.
Matthew 11:28 (NIV)

During the Alpha course, the participants hear talks about the Bible, prayer, faith, Jesus, God and the Holy Spirit. It is interesting to observe how people respond during the 11 weeks. They show a lot of interest and participate in discussions and toss around many questions. What I have noticed is that nothing seems to quite make sense until the moment they understand why Jesus died. This glues it all together. It is so precious to witness how their eyes light up as they step into a new life. (*Stepping through the Stargate JC*). Jesus is the key to all. Until people can understand the reason of His death and resurrection, nothing will make sense to them.

As previously mentioned, I was raised as a Catholic. By then the mass was spoken in our language, but during the time my mother grew up, it was all spoken in Latin. She had to go to church every morning before school. I wonder if the kids caught up on their homework or played naughts & crosses to pass the time? It must have been awfully boring, even for the adults, standing there and pretending to understand. It doesn't make sense to hold a mass when one is unable to follow what is being said and prayed. It demonstrated to me that we 'ordinary folks' were not good enough for God. Latin was just another curtain that was put up to signify the power of the church, instead of following what Jesus has taught us.

I believe this could also be a reason why the Catholics, as well as other denominations encourage people to pray to Saints. In other words, they pray indirectly to God, rather than directly, as we ought to. This reminds me of a somewhat amusing memory of mine as I was growing up:

Every night my parents would pray with us when we were very little. So when I was a bit older I tried to pray before I went to sleep every night. How I started my prayers resembled the way one would address people before a speech or writing a letter. I took this very seriously and didn't want to insult any of my favourite saints by not including their names. I did love them. Then I also had to consider all the loved ones that passed away, especially my father. I would start my prayer like Dear God, dear Saint…, dear Saint… and the list would go on and on. In many instances I didn't even 'make' it through to the actual prayer, because I fell asleep before I could finish going through my long list. Often I would give the prayers a miss. I found it a tad daunting and a bit boring to start with. But, I did stay awake sometimes and still got to pray…

I cannot recall if anyone ever told me that I had to pray this way, I just did. Even during my childhood I had the impression that there was the church and there was us. To pray to a Saint seemed the right way for me. They were closer than God. God was too immense and distant. I think that somehow I was influenced in such a way that I either didn't feel worthy to speak to God directly or that I felt that He was out of my reach. This false conviction stuck with me for many years.

Both sides of the family were very strong believers in God, but also in the Saints. Every Saint was known to help in certain areas of need. I heard and read of so many testimonies of people who were healed by Saints. Many stories also tell how Saints help people in difficult situations.

One day I misplaced the house keys and I was told that I was grounded until I would find them. All day I was searching everywhere, but couldn't find them. Mum would have observed that even with my best efforts I couldn't find the keys. So she walked over to the church, prayed and put some money into the donation box for Saint Anthony. When she came back, she knew exactly where the keys were. She walked straight to the letterbox and grabbed them from there. I didn't think much of it then, but felt relief and I was finally free to go and join the other kids. I guess in hindsight it was a miracle.

Now it has all changed for me. I start my prayers with: Dear God, dear Jesus, dear Father in Heaven, dear Lord or Holy Spirit. In chapter 'Who is God' we can find many other ways in which we can address God in our prayers. It is much easier this way and I can get on with what I want to say to God without drifting off to sleep beforehand. I think God doesn't mind by what name we call Him, as long as we keep in touch with Him every day. All this, Jesus has made possible for us.

Some denominations, like the Baptists, don't pray to the Saints. In the beginning I couldn't quite understand the reason. One day I had a long chat to a lady during a course held at church. She was very adamant that we ought to only pray to God, not to anyone else. In the beginning of our conversation I started to carefully put my point of view across but then I began to realise what she really meant. Through Jesus, we have direct access to God and there is no need for any intercessors. God is not as far away as we sometimes tend to believe. He is right here with us and if we are willing, within us.

Why the Cross?

During the rule of the Roman Empire, only the worst criminals and the lowest of the lowest were executed by crucifixion. Therefore no set rules were set in place and the executioners did as they pleased. The crosses were put up along the main roads leading into Jerusalem or other cities. Everyone going to and fro had to pass by. Crucifixion was not only heinous and gruesome, it also was humiliating and degrading to hang there naked for everyone to be stared at, spat on and laughed at whilst suffering excruciating pain and dying.

It can be difficult to understand the extent and significance of the death of Jesus. Why did they have to torture Him in such horrid ways? Could this not have been avoided? However, would His death and ministry have made such an impact on this world as it has? Would anyone still remember who Jesus is? Sadly, Jesus is more famous for His sufferings and cruel death than His miracles. The cross has become the trademark of Jesus and signifies Christianity.

Suffering and enduring this kind of execution only meant for the worst criminals and outlaws. Jesus, who bore no sin, humbled Himself for us and verified His love to all humankind. He knew what would happen to Him from the beginning. Many times He conveyed to His apostles that He would be taken away.

17 Now Jesus was going up to Jerusalem. On the way, he took the Twelve aside and said to them,
18 "We are going up to Jerusalem, and the Son of Man will be delivered over to the chief priests and the teachers of the law. They will condemn him to death
19 and will hand him over to the Gentiles to be mocked and flogged and crucified. On the third day he will be raised to life!"
Matthew 20:17-19 (NIV)

Jesus also mentioned this earlier on in the Gospel of Matthew, 17:22-23. He could have simply bailed out and disappeared. But He endured the pain and humiliation to give us back our freedom, to make us right with God our Father. Now the question remains of why the death of Jesus was so significant. Could God not just forgive us? Why was the suffering and death irrefutably necessary? This has always been a question that I have been wrestling with. It is something that is not easy to understand but once you do, your life will change and never be the same again. At that moment you will ask yourself how you managed to live your life without Jesus.

In his letter to the Corinthian church, Paul has wonderfully described it as 'we are a new Creation':

> 17 Therefore, if anyone is in Christ, the new Creation has come: The old has gone, the new is here!
> 18 All this is from God, who reconciled us to himself through Christ and gave us the ministry of reconciliation:
> 19 that God was reconciling the world to himself in Christ, not counting people's sins against them. And he has committed to us the message of reconciliation.
> 2 Corinthians 5:17-19 (NIV)

Christianity hinges on the death and resurrection of Jesus. Without it, there is no purpose. Apart from His teachings and healing, the sole purpose of Jesus was to reconnect and reconcile us with God. This was only possible through His death. When He died, it appeared as if Jesus was defeated, but through His resurrection however, He conquered death and the evil of this world. It is also vital to look at the last seven statements Jesus made whilst dying on the cross as they bear deep meaning.

1. Jesus said, **"Father, forgive them, for they do not know what they are doing."** Luke 23:34 (NIV)
Despite all the pain and humiliation inflicted on Him, His first concern remained with all humankind. He tells us to forgive

others as God forgives us. The other very important point to note is that Jesus was still connected to His Father in Heaven.

2   *Jesus answered him,* ***"Truly I tell you, today you will be with me in paradise."*** *Luke 23:43 (NIV)*
One of the two criminals that were crucified with Jesus recognised and believed in Jesus. He asked Him to remember him. Jesus immediately welcomes Him to the family of God. He showed us that it is never too late to reconsider our actions and change course. We all can be forgiven if we choose, it is all up to us.

3.   *And at three in the afternoon Jesus cried out in a loud voice, "Eloi, Eloi, lemasabachthani?" (which means* ***"My God, my God, why have you forsaken me?"****). Mark 15:34 (NIV)*
This was the very moment when Jesus took every sin of all humankind upon Himself so that even His father in Heaven turned His face away from Him. Up to this time, Jesus was always connected with His Father and He had never been alone. But at this very juncture He was totally disconnected, left all alone on the cross during His worst and most agonising hour.

4.   *26 When Jesus saw his mother there, and the disciple whom he loved standing nearby, he said to her,* ***"Woman, here is your son,"***
    27 and to the disciple, ***"Here is your mother."*** *From that time on, this disciple took her into his home. John 19:26-27 (NIV)*
Looking at His weeping widowed mother, Jesus made sure that she would be taken care of. He committed her to His favourite apostle, John. His concern still remained for others. He also tells us to take care of each other, no matter in what circumstances we find ourselves in.

5.   *Later, knowing that everything had now been finished, and so that Scripture would be fulfilled, Jesus said,* ***"I am thirsty."*** *John 19:28 (NIV)*
To His last breath, Jesus made sure He followed the will of His

Father, as it was prophesied in the OT (Psalm 69:21: *They put gall in my food and gave me vinegar for my thirst.)*

6. *When he had received the drink, Jesus said,* **"It is finished."** *With that, he bowed his head and gave up his spirit. John 19:30 (NIV)*
Jesus tells us that He has now cleared the way for us. He has conquered evil and opened the gates of Heaven for everyone who wishes to be reunited with God.

7. *Jesus called out with a loud voice,* **"Father, into your hands I commit my spirit."** *Luke 23:46 (NIV)*
Here Jesus is finally released from His physical and emotional sufferings and returns home.

Jesus came to demonstrate what true love and forgiveness is. In His love for all humankind, He endured crucifixion and death. This portrays the true character of God, the picture of true love. His resurrection illustrates the real power of God to raise the dead and the power of love. As a result, we receive the opportunity to follow Jesus. We will stay alive just as the criminal on the cross next to Jesus did. It does not matter what we have done in life up until this very moment. When we ask for and trust the coordinates of the Stargate JC and step through, the 'old' is left behind forever.

Yes, Jesus is our hope and the light of the world. There really is nothing else that compares. Jesus gives us back the confidence to tackle all of life's challenges. We can always turn to Him in our darkest hour and He will be there with His protection, guidance, wisdom and most of all, His love.

For I can do everything through Christ, who gives me strength. Philippians 4:13 (NLT)

Once you have found Jesus, you will never be alone again. You will stop searching and never be craving for love again. Jesus will give you all you need in abundance.

I remember when I turned forty. I had a secure and well-paid job and seemed to have everything I needed. But often I would lie in my bed, asking myself why I wasn't happy? There I was, in my own house, with a new car in the garage, a motorbike parked outside, many good friends and a steady job. I should be out there having the time of my life. But instead I was slowly sinking into a slight depression, saddened by the fact that the only thing that was missing in my life was love. I was convinced that if I were able to find the right partner, my life would be complete. There was only one drawback that stood in the way: I was not in control. Anything else I was able to achieve or buy, but not love. If only I knew then what I know now. But then, it is never too late.

Since I started to go to church and learned more and more about Jesus, my loneliness slowly dissolved and was replaced with an inner peace and contentment. I don't feel lonely anymore. I now have a purpose in life and am happy. Whenever I need help, I call Jesus for help. Whenever I encounter a special moment, I call Jesus to share my joy with and thank Him. I have a strong sense of security and belonging. When I watch or read the news, I get upset over the state of this world and pray that people would start to open their hearts and seek God. I wish everyone could feel the way I do.

Jesus gives me the freedom to do what I need to do without having to answer to anyone. I often refer to God as my boss and point my finger up to heaven. It may sound funny and people are often laughing, but this is exactly how I feel. Jesus has given me a new lease on life. For this reason I got baptised and asked Jesus to be in my life and that I wanted to follow Him. With baptism, we get fully immersed in water, which symbolises the death of the old life and the cleansing. As we emerge from the water, we are set free and can begin a new life.

Peter replied, "Repent and be baptised, every one of you, in the name of Jesus Christ for the forgiveness of your sins. And you will receive the gift of the Holy Spirit.
Acts 2:38 (NIV)

It really is a simple as that. Jesus is not complicated, we are. All you need to do is to take stock (repent) of your life and recognise what actions or ways of thinking don't correspond with God; meaning, any conduct and attitude with the absence of love. There is no need to judge others and to carry grudges. All you need to do is focus on your own actions. You are not responsible nor in control of other people's behaviour. Therefore you can leave them with God. This lightens your burden when you encounter difficult situations. Most of all, forgive others as God forgives you. This will set you free.

Never look back, but set your focus on your future. Nothing that you have done in the past will change your future. Rather what you are doing right now is what will affect your future. As the saying goes, don't cry over spilled milk, wipe it off and move on. God is only interested in what you are doing from here on in.

So the word repent can be best translated to *acknowledge, regret, feel remorse* or *change and leave the past behind.*

We need to reassess ourselves (die) and dispose of the bad stuff (repent) on a daily basis. The apostle Paul puts it like this:

20 I have been crucified with Christ and I no longer live, but Christ lives in me. The life I now live in the body, I live by faith in the Son of God, who loved me and gave himself for me. 21 I do not set aside the grace of God, for if righteousness could be gained through the law, Christ died for nothing!"
Galatians 2:20-21 (NIV)

In times of distress, grief, loss, despair or ill health, people look for someone for support them and to draw strength from. These are the times when the hearts, eyes and ears are being opened, ready to cast their attention toward the *spiritual* world and remove the focus from the *worldly* world. There we find the true answers. God uses these times to draw people back to Him.

My prayer 19.01.14

"Dear Jesus please strengthen my relationship with you. Wrap a rope tightly around us so that nothing can draw me away from you and that I cannot go astray on my walk with you."

Amen

Sins dissolved through Jesus

Sins are things we should avoid doing as it inflicts harm to others, the future and even to ourselves. Sin can also be described as an action that is against the law of the universe. As humans, we are not perfect and will always succumb to human weaknesses. Thus, it leaves our souls tarnished and unable to resonate with God's frequency: the light of love. This is what makes it impossible to be fully connected to our Creator. God is the Creator of all, therefore He can see ahead of all times. Time does not exist for Him; He is the great **I AM**. He sees all our future deeds. He forgives us before we even sin. He sent us Jesus as the intercessor to show us the way and lead us back to Him.

Jesus said: "*I am the truth*". He, if we believe in him, can cleanse our souls. It means that our sins are forgiven and we have the ability to tune back into God's frequency in accordance with His laws. Jesus showed us how we can get a ticket back to the Garden of Eden. Only through Him can we begin to see the truth and be filled with peace and joy that no money can buy. His light fills our hearts with true happiness. Earthly possessions such as money, luxury cars, mansions or power only produce temporary happiness, whereas the peace of God lasts an eternity. None of our possessions and achievements has any worth in the afterlife nor does it get us there.

Yes, only by faith in Jesus can our sins be dissolved and our souls released so that they may no longer remain trapped in darkness.

When Jesus spoke again to the people, he said, "I am the light of the world. Whoever follows me will never walk in darkness, but will have the light of life."
John 8:12 (NIV)

While I am in the world, I am the light of the world."
John 9:5 (NIV)

Yet I am writing you a new command; its truth is seen in Him and in you, because the darkness is passing and the true light is already shining.
1John 2:8 (NIV)

When we pass on, we will be able to reconnect with our Creator. This is what it means to be part of His Kingdom. I believe that all human beings have eternal life since we all have souls, which don't die. The question is, what sort of eternal life would you like to lead and where do you want to end up? We only have the choice of two directions. There is neither a middle way nor a halfway house. You are either with or against God.

There are those who accept Jesus and who will be saved. I can just imagine how Jesus is picking us up at the 'Pearly Gates' and taking us straight to the Kingdom of God. With Him, we will be in the light, surrounded by eternal love.

Then there are the ones who are against God. They will not be saved and go the opposite direction. Where will their souls be 'roaming around'? The question is how long will a soul endure in darkness, cut off from the power source of the Creator? Not a very inspiring deliberation. The Bible describes this place as hell. There is no bliss, only agony, turmoil and disorder, a forsaken domain ruled by Satan.

17 He came and preached peace to you who were far away and peace to those who were near.
18 For through him we both have access to the Father by one Spirit.
19 Consequently, you are no longer foreigners and strangers,

but fellow citizens with God's people and also members of his household,
20 built on the foundation of the apostles and prophets, with Christ Jesus himself as the chief cornerstone.
21 In him the whole building is joined together and rises to become a holy temple in the LORD.
22 And in him you too are being built together to become a dwelling in which God lives by his Spirit.
Ephesians 2:17-22 (NIV)

This defines who Jesus is, what he has done and why:

15 The Son is the image of the invisible God, the firstborn over all Creation.
16 For in him all things were created: things in heaven and on Earth, visible and invisible, whether thrones or powers or rulers or authorities; all things have been created through him and for him.
17 He is before all things, and in him all things hold together.
18 And he is the head of the body, the church; he is the beginning and the firstborn from among the dead, so that in everything he might have the supremacy.
19 For God was pleased to have all his fullness dwell in him,
20 and through him to reconcile to himself all things, whether things on Earth or things in heaven, by making peace through his blood, shed on the cross. 21 Once you were alienated from God and were enemies in your minds because of your evil behaviour.
22 But now he has reconciled you by Christ's physical body through death to present you holy in his sight, without blemish and free from accusation
Colossians 1:15-22 (NIV)

The Ice Box

*"**O**nce upon a time there was a man. We'll call him Billy. He was very excited since he was looking forward to the BBQ party that he had been planning for the past few days. An hour before the guests were to arrive, to his dismay, he realises that he totally forgot about the ice. So he sets out to try to find some close by. To his surprise, he spots a man standing across the road with free ice to give away. Billy's spirit takes a leap and he counts himself very lucky. He runs to fetch this bargain. The man at the stall asks him for an icebox to put the ice into it. Billy realises that he had come unprepared. He still accepts the free ice and makes his way back home. By the time he gets home, half the ice had already melted. Again, Billy is not too worried and opens the freezer to place the ice in, but there was no room left. It was filled to the brim with stuff that he had accumulated over time. He had a choice to either throw some old stuff out to make room or just not to worry about the ice. So he decides to let the ice melt, as it would have taken too much effort to clear out the freezer. Billy is not too worried; the ice was for free anyway..."*

Are you too looking for ice (Salvation) for your BBQ party (life)? Here stands Jesus (the man) and offers you the best ice, absolutely for free. But there is a slight problem; you have no icebox (belief) to take it home with. You have not prepared yourself and brought the icebox along with you. Even if you were to take the free gift (ice) home, without faith you cannot hold on to it too long. Whatever is left needs to be placed in the freezer (your heart) very quickly. Have you cleared out (repented) the 'stuff' that you won't need anymore? Have you made room for the new (get baptised)?

Grace, salvation and the forgiveness of God are a free gift that is on offer to all of us. All we have to do is say yes and accept it. It sounds very simple and one wonders why not everyone would take up such an offer. There is one little catch; we need faith and to have faith we must believe and to believe we must let go of our 'old' ways first.

For some of you, this chapter may have made sense and you now understand who Jesus is. Perhaps you are ready to respond and commence a new chapter in your life. Would you like to receive this free gift from Jesus?

There is a simple prayer that you can pray to accept Jesus in your life as your Lord and Saviour right now. It is very short but powerful and takes effect immediately. Jesus will not let you wait. This prayer can be prayed in various similar ways, but the principle remains the same.

This is the salvation prayer we use at Alpha:

Lord Jesus Christ,

I am sorry for the things I have done wrong in my life.

(Take a few moments here to ask for His forgiveness for anything particular that is in your heart)

Please forgive me. I now turn from everything which I know is wrong.

Thank you that you died on the cross for me so that I could be forgiven and set free.

Thank you that you now offer me this gift of forgiveness
and Your Spirit.
I now receive that gift.

Please come into my life by Your Holy Spirit to be with me forever.

Thank you Lord Jesus

Amen

Which points right back to the core of the apple…Jesus, our Lord and Saviour

God's Kingdom - How do I get there?

Since the beginning of time, the biggest enigma has always been that of the existence of an afterlife and a God. Some deny the existence of God and therefore convince themselves that death is the end of the line, whereas others believe in God or other spirits and an afterlife.

The Egyptians and many other cultures buried their dead with all their accumulated treasures, food, weapons, livestock and anything they would need in the afterlife. Some cultures would even entomb their wives and servants with them. These rituals indicate to what extent people would go to, out of fear of death, subsequently the 'unknown'. We have no control over death and neither can we avoid it. When the time is up, it is up. There is no certainty nor do we get a practice run. Life is here and now and the end is undisclosed to us. We cannot return and try again. No one has ever come back and to tell the tale. What we will find out is that leading a life of long-term thinking is the right choice. A Christian life revolves around a long-term focus and beyond. What is longer, life on Earth or life in the spiritual domain? Our thoughts and actions will have consequences and it is wise to keep them in check.

Whilst driving to work one morning, I was unprepared to what was to happen. Unexpectedly an amazing sentence popped to mind. God revealed to me an insight of what life is like in His Kingdom. It often happens that God surprises me with the most brilliant messages when I least expect it. These profound words still give me goose bumps. They represent the end goal, the promise of God. This is what is in store for us and what Jesus promises to us all. We just have to say yes.

Concerned that I might forget, I quickly jotted down the sentence on a scrap of paper and slipped it in the side pocket of my car door. When I set out to write this book I gathered all my notes and bits and pieces that I knew I had stashed away everywhere; on my desk, in drawers, in the kitchen, in the car, in books and handbag.

Months later when I read this particular note again, to my dismay, I couldn't decipher my own handwriting. One word looked like it could have been two words. No matter what I tried, I couldn't make it out. I was unable to remember the exact wording, as it was definitely not in my own style of writing.

Then at last I recalled that the Bible tells us that we don't have to rely on our own wisdom. This was the perfect moment to find out if God would really step in. With true conviction I said: "God, these are your words, please open my eyes so that I can read them clearly." Immediately the words appeared so distinctly. In fact, I could hardly believe that I was unable to read them in the first place. It goes to show that God is always present. He has demonstrated to me that all we have to do is ask...and here is the 'eminent' sentence:

"Eternal life is to live in love; a constant eternal bliss in the existence of total truth."

To experience the full glory of God is the ultimate fulfillment of eternal life, but this is only possible in our spiritual existence. On another occasion during a morning walk, I must have been reflecting on what life would be like after death. This is what came to mind:

"God's kingdom is like a choir, we all will sing in tune and harmony. Jesus taught us here on Earth, how to sing in unison. We need to adjust to His tune to create the ultimate, divine and perfect melody. I could nearly make out a most amazing melody that was accompanied by beautiful colours that don't even exist here on Earth.
In this world, people are trying to sing a song together, but no one is willing to harmonise. Everyone sings their own chords without taking notice of one another, not to mention the conductor (God). No wonder we have such disharmony

and disorder. People are focused on perfecting their own song, rather than perfecting the collective song. We all belong to ONE and the same choir."

Could it be that humankind has always been in search for such a blissful utopian melody? Only, they never quite knew what it is and are left with emptiness inside. It can never be found unless we listen to what Jesus has passed on to us in His parables and teachings. Then we can begin to understand and start our pursuit of the ultimate fulfillment, the final unison with our Creator. No longer will there be loneliness, confusion and emptiness.

"Speaking to one another with psalms, hymns, and songs from the Spirit.
Sing and make music from your heart to the LORD,"
Ephesians 5:19 (NIV)

My Prayer:

Dear LORD, may Your song echo in my heart forever and ever.
Amen

Last year I was talking with a very good friend of mine. As we often do, we got engaged in a 'God Talk'. Amongst many topics we discussed eternal life. With a sudden clarity I began to understand what Jesus is telling us through His parables of which I have already touched on in chapter "Did Jesus die for us".

"We can only achieve eternal life, which is a promise of Jesus, by removing all darkness from our soul (being). We need to be pure in the spirit. One must be completely in the light, which is God. We have to <u>fine-tune our soul</u> to the correct specifications given to us by God. If we follow His ways

(commands) we can tweak our soul and inner being back to God's likeness and 'frequency' so that we can re-enter His domain.

Our energy must be able to flow freely just like the water flows through a pipe. If the water is dirty, the pipe will get blocked up and the flow slows down and stops. We get overpowered by darkness and get 'clogged up' by allowing evil to tempt and persuade us to choose worldly pursuits over spiritual pursuits. As long as we hold on to Jesus, we are safe and evil has no hold over us. Sin is the impurity that puts a barrier between God and us. (Refer to Chapter "Why not sin")"

During my writing, I have encountered the same predicament over and over again; some insights and ideas are being repeated in different chapters. I often wrestle with what version to keep in which chapter. But I believe different versions talk to different people. I also feel that it is important and ok to reiterate on a subject, just as the Bible keeps repeating the messages across the Old and New Testament.

There needs to be love in our heart to establish a two-way communication with God (1st Commandment). A few years ago whilst driving along, not thinking of anything in particular, I heard a gentle voice saying these words: *"We communicate with you through love, which serves as a telephone line to you".* Well, you can imagine how stunned I was. But it did make sense, even at a time in my life when I was not in touch with God. But God never lost touch with me (Chapter 'How did I find God'). The car seems to be a great place for me to 'hang out' with God...it works well for me.

From whatever angle we look at, it all points back to love. God is love and light. We are capable to be just like this too. Our pure essence is trapped deep within us, suppressed by impurities, derived from worldly desires that are only short-lived. The flame of our soul has diminished to the size of a pilot light; threatened to be extinguished. More than ever do we need Jesus to rekindle our flame to shine brightly again. Through Jesus we can re-ignite our love and share it with the rest of the world.

In so many ways God is telling us that there is no other

than Him. He has created us, therefore desires only the best for us. So He sent Jesus to open up the Stargate to pave a way home for us.

To worship anything or anyone else is to no avail and pointless. The same applies to leading a self-centred and superficial life. It distracts our attention from the true essence of life. We only waste our time on empty promises.

The Spirit of Jesus revealed to the apostle John what life in the Kingdom of God is like. We find this in the last book of the New Testament:

3 And I heard a loud voice from the throne saying, "Look! God's dwelling place is now among the people, and he will dwell with them. They will be his people, and God himself will be with them and be their God.
4 'He will wipe every tear from their eyes. There will be no more death' or mourning or crying or pain, for the old order of things has passed away."
5 He who was seated on the throne said, "I am making everything new!"
Revelation 21:3-5 (NIV)

Following verses of Psalm 81 spoke to me. God must often get sad watching from His world how we aimlessly and blindly stumble and fumble through life like lost 'sheep', searching for answers in all the wrong places. God keeps showing us the way but we continue to look the opposite way.

8 Hear me, my people, and I will warn you—
if you would only listen to me, Israel!
9 You shall have no foreign god among you;
you shall not worship any god other than me.
10 I am the LORD your God,
who brought you up out of Egypt.
Open wide your mouth and I will fill it.

11 "But my people would not listen to me;
Israel would not submit to me.

12 So I gave them over to their stubborn hearts
to follow their own devices.

13 "If my people would only listen to me,
if Israel would only follow my ways,
14 how quickly I would subdue their enemies
and turn my hand against their foes!
15 Those who hate the LORD would cringe before him,
and their punishment would last forever.
16 But you would be fed with the finest of wheat;
with honey from the rock I would satisfy you."
Psalm 81:8-16 (NIV)

Why do we repeatedly ignore history, instead of learning from it? We continue to allow our past to become our future. On one of my visits to my mother's hometown, we went to have a look at a very old mausoleum. You could also call it a chapel of remembrance. Secured behind bars, hundreds of sculls are stacked up against the wall. Above on a timber beam, it reads the following inscription:

"What you are now, is what we were"
———————
"What we are today, is what you will become"

For some, it may be a bit scary to look at human sculls. The mind starts to wonder what happened to these people and what kind of life they had. Nevertheless, the inscription is what has impressed me most and it never left my mind. It came to mind whilst writing this book as it fits in well. There is wisdom in these words, but I can also detect a certain undertone of defeat. Could they also be read like this?

'This is what it is, but does not have to be so. But if willing, we can change who and what we are and will become.'

Let us reconsider our actions today, as we want to look

forward to a different tomorrow. Look at the past for lessons, not for lamentations and criticism. Instead, we ought to take heed of the shortfalls of our ancestors so as not to step into the same trap.

A few years back I read that in business, one should first research on where and how other businesses and entrepreneurs have failed. Then strategise new ideas that have not yet been tried before. It will save valuable time and money. It is more profitable and predictable to take advantage of other people's failures rather than trying to come up with new ideas that may have already been tried. Why not learn from where others have failed. Alfred Einstein's famous definition of insanity sums it up perfectly:

*"**Insanity**: doing the same thing over and over again and expecting different results."*

As I carried on with my 'Bible in one year' programme, repeatedly I discovered that all the answers are already in the Bible. There is no denying of how much wisdom can be found in the Bible. In fact, it contains all the wisdom we need. It simply outlines the laws and principles of the universe, just like the law of gravity. It all has to be in a certain order to be able to function in perfect harmony.

Pursuing inconsequential dreams and goals in life will have their repercussions. Each one of us has a free will, and therefore bears the responsibility of the choices made and the actions taken. There is no one else to blame.

Can we really AFFORD to continue to be *against God*? Alternatively, is it time for us to reflect and begin to realign our compass to God? What is your current setting on your navigator? What do you want your long term future to look like? Are you prepared to step out of your comfort zone and take a different direction?

Consequent verses written by the apostle Paul encompass the principle message of this book. When I first read this passage, I went over it a few times to make sure that I got it right. I could have literally deleted everything I had written so far and just 'published' these verses. This is the core of Paul's message to the world. It surprises me that it's not quoted more often. You too may have to read it several times.

11 So Christ himself gave the apostles, the prophets, the evangelists, the pastors and teachers,
12 to equip his people for works of service, so that the body of Christ may be built up
13 until we all reach unity in the faith and in the knowledge of the Son of God and become mature, attaining to the whole measure of the fullness of Christ.
14 Then we will no longer be infants, tossed back and forth by the waves, and blown here and there by every wind of teaching and by the cunning and craftiness of people in their deceitful scheming.
15 Instead, speaking the truth in love, we will grow to become in every respect the mature body of him who is the head, that is, Christ.
16 From him the whole body, joined and held together by every supporting ligament, grows and builds itself up in love, as each part does its work.
Ephesians 4:11-16 (NIV)

Amazingly, these verses point towards and validate what we read earlier on: *"Eternal life is to live in love; a constant eternal bliss in the existence of total truth."*

How can we accomplish this? How do we get to the Kingdom of God? The only way is through Jesus, our 'Stargate'. And this is how:

The Decision: is **the Match** you need to start your fire burning. You will only need one match e.g. you only make the decision once. (At the end of chapter "Did Jesus die for us" you can find the prayer to invite Jesus into your life)

The Commitment: is to **Get Started by Gathering** kindling and use your match to get your fire burning.

Jesus: is **the Wood** that keeps the fire burning strong, withstanding the torrents of life and gives shelter when it rains. The more 'Jesus' you apply and the longer you keep at it, the bigger and stronger your fire will burn.
The size of your flame reflects the depth of relationship you have with God, the kind of quality of life you lead and the strength of your faith. At the end of your days, God will remember your strong fire. With Jesus you will enter the Kingdom of God and your 'soul' will burn on forever.

Which points right back to the core of the apple…Jesus, who gives eternal life

Why not Sin?

What is Sin?

The search result for the word "sin" in the OT and NT combined comes up with an astonishing 414 times (NET version). Repetitions always indicate that a particular subject IS important.

What does *Sin* actually mean? Does *Sin* represent: "*Harming yourself and/or others; disrupting harmony peace?*" Could committing or not committing sin determine *the outcome of our spiritual future*? Indeed, this calls us to weigh up our conduct with great care.

Nonetheless, there are distinct layers to consider. Sins contain all actions that do not agree with the spiritual laws; hence, they are not in accordance to God's dimension. Every sin is generated by negative energy, and without exception followed by negative consequences. By us ignoring God's guidelines, we are in fact challenging the spiritual laws. In other words, to commit a sin and then consider it to be ok equates to jumping off a tall building, trying to defy the law of gravity. In either case, it can only result in a 'crash landing'.

James (brother of Jesus) puts it like this:

14 but each person is tempted when they are dragged away by their own evil desire and enticed.
15 Then, after desire has conceived, it gives birth to sin; and sin, when it is full-grown, gives birth to death.
16 Don't be deceived, my dear brothers and sisters.
James 1:14-15 (NIV)

Sin is a word that has been chosen to describe such actions. It sounds condemning and does not correspond with our so-called modern way of life. In addition, the word sin elicits a picture of 'burning in hell'. Naturally, this image does not resonate too well. Human nature tends to side step in order to avoid inner conflict. In this case they make believe that 'sin' is outdated, overrated and irrelevant, therefore dismiss sin as a scare tactic. It is much easier to look the other way and be blinded and distracted by the glitter and glamour of the world we know. It comes with instant gratification, but lacks a long term view.

I dare to take this even a step further. One evening a very clear thought came to mind. If we were to trace our steps back, right to the very beginning, the Creation. Could we be as bold as to assert that love is the summation of all emotions and energies? This then would include both, negative and positive. Just what the Bible tells us, God is pure love and has created everything there is. Subsequently, Evil is also a part of Creation.

However, the strength and power of evil is determined by our sins. The more we give in to sin, the stronger evil will grow. Therefore evil is the summation of all sin. Sins are the result of thoughts that are driven by our desires. These desires are derived from the temptations and persuasions that Satan casts upon us. Satan, who used to be an angel, is referred to as Lucifer (*morning star* or *day star*) the *fallen angel* (see Isaiah 14:12). He intended to rise above God but then was cast down to Earth. In order to build his own empire here on Earth, he seduces humankind in order to draw us away from God. He is brilliant and conniving at making the *bad* look innocent and harmless and the *good* to appear unworthy and useless. Therefore, people do not realise this until it is too late and have to endure the consequences of which I will elaborate further in the following subchapter, 'Why not sin'.

To state that evil is part of Creation is a rather confronting statement, but humans sin and are part of Creation. For some of you it may sound a bit too farfetched and may raise and eyebrow or two. Now we ask ourselves why God would create evil. The logical conclusion would be that everything that exists must have an opposite pole, good and evil, positive and negative, black and white, light and dark. For instance, if there is no heat there can also be no cold. This explains that love encompasses everything. However, it is all created to interface within the correct balance. Love is and will always remain the strongest force, capable of anything. It can overcome all things, including evil, which is the accumulation of sin.

Yes, why did God make evil part of Creation? Would it not be perfect if there were no evil in the first place? Then there would be no war, violence, crime or pain. For anything to function and harmonise, there must be an opposite that creates the necessary tension. Electricity would not work without a positive and negative pole. There has to be an exchange of reaction, just as good and bad. Without good there cannot be bad. Without light there cannot be darkness. Without water there cannot be ice. How would you be able to conceive the idea of what silence is if you have no sound? Without the mountains, there are no valleys.

At this point, our freewill comes into play. For example, a mother tells her little toddler not to touch the hot stove. It is up to the child to either touch it or trust the mother and stay clear. We too have a choice: *to sin or not to sin*. Like a toddler, we can either burn our fingers by ignoring God's warnings or trust and stay safe. The good news is that through Jesus our sins are forgiven. When we have made the wrong choice (sin) and learned from it, we can reform (repent) and start afresh. We all make mistakes in life, but some of us choose to continue and repeat the same mistakes in total ignorance. Many get trapped with temptations and addictions. The one thing that can release us from this vicious and deadly cycle is to have faith in Jesus. We can either listen to our Creator or fumble around and get burned by our wrongdoings, our sins.

We also have to take into account that without good and evil there would be no need for a free will. Our free will stands in between good and evil. Existence as we know it would not be possible without the constant friction of choices. From the Bible we learn that we are given a free will. By that, it verifies the existence and necessity of the two poles: good and evil, light and dark, positive and negative, ugly and beautiful. It also explains that there are only two choices available; either it is with or without God; to sin or not to sin.

Whilst I was contemplating whether I could include these thoughts, my hand began to draw an illustration on a scrap of paper. After looking at it for a moment, I realised that it portrayed a visual explanation. I was then encouraged to go ahead with 'my' theory of what sin is:

God - **Us** (Free Will) - **Evil**

* **God** is (**I AM**), unchangeable, perfect and
<u>**consistent**</u>

* **Us,** the only variable element in the equation
<u>**unpredictable**</u>

* **Evil** will feed off our vulnerability, pride, egocentricity,
ignorance and greed
<u>**predictable**</u>

It does not allow room for any grey areas. It is very important to identify why God has given us so many warnings, right through from the OT to the NT.

It can be confusing and rather frightening to read about the *wrath* of God. Is not God described as being gentle, loving, forgiving and kind? How then can He turn His *wrath* against us? His severe warnings reflect just how strong His love for us is. They are meant to be taken seriously and not for us to be scared of God. He warns us that our choices, decisions and actions will set the course of our journey beyond.

It does not suffice to proclaim to believe in God and evil and at the same time remain in middle, the neutral zone. There is no such thing. The day will come when a decision has to be made. What is stopping us from doing so today? Let us be consistent rather than just being the unpredictable variable element, which can be so easily swayed into the wrong direction.

Our existence is interwoven with the universe; one cannot exist without the other. This perfect but complex cycle of Creation connects all aspects of life. Our intellectual capacity and intelligence is incapable of comprehending the expansive laws of the spiritual reality as opposed to the virtual reality in which we live in. It is not a necessity to have all the answers to our questions. However, we need to be fully aware that a compromise in the spiritual dimension is not possible. In other words, the laws of this world are not applicable in the spiritual world. Our choices today determine how each of us will spend our eternal life. In this lifetime we must graduate from spiritual infants to becoming mature and prepared to enter a realm that we cannot possibly fathom. The closest we can ever get to experience a spiritual law is when we witness a supernatural phenomenon, which we also refer to as a miracle of God. It cannot be physically explained. We find many such incidents in the Bible as well as in today's time when certain people have received a gift of healing, speaking an unknown language, can prophesy or achieve the impossible. All these can only be possible through God.

Yes, miracles do still happen. There are other instances where we are allowed to get a glimpse into the spiritual world.

One of these moments I described in chapter "How Did I Find God". All I can remember is that during this amazing split second I knew exactly how God connects to all of us at the same time. I recall that it all made perfect sense. Unfortunately, these enlightenments only last a few seconds and then vanish. Isn't the assurance of the presence and love of God what really matters?

Which points right back to the core of the apple…God, our Guardian over good and bad

The Ten Commandments

No matter what dimension we find ourselves in, specific laws govern all elements. For example the law of gravity, procreation, weather patterns, day and night, seasons, rotation of planets around the sun or the influence of the moon on our oceans, are only a few that apply to Earth. It all interacts as a whole. If you were to dismiss only one of these laws, Earth and life, as we know it, would cease to exist.

However, gravity does not exist in God's spiritual dimension, nor is there any need to sleep or eat. It operates under different laws. We may also call them 'The 10 Commandments'. These laws are the guidelines of God's dimension, a non-material realm. It is necessary for us to understand that these commandments are not here to restrict us. On the contrary, they are in place to provide us with a passageway to our Creator. Each Commandment is a safety rail, which keeps us from slipping. Unfortunately, some people perceive them as being outdated and choose to live by their own laws without considering the implications of the long term effects.

These Commandments are not nor will they ever be outdated. Life is a collective event. On the worldly side, we have time restrictions, whereas the spiritual domain exists in a timeless space. By nature, we humans only tend to think of what we can do whilst we are alive. Instead, we ought to projecting the outcome of our actions into infinity.

Each one of us is a small drop in the ocean, but without these drops, there cannot be an ocean either. Maybe it is time to re-evaluate the importance of the individual part we each play in the collective existence.

I felt the need to dust the cobwebs off the Ten Commandments. They have a reason to be there, all ten of them. Our sense of self-confidence and self-reliance prevents us from taking the Ten Commandments to heart. We tend to consider them a hindrance that only constricts us from what we want. Rather, we ought to acknowledge them as support and guidance in our daily life. The Ten Commandments symbolise the blueprint of God's Realm. If they were adhered to, we could have Heaven on Earth, a perfect world, as perfect as God.

Imagine yourself walking along an overhanging cliff. No warning signs are put up to make you aware of any danger nor are there any handrails to keep you steady. A strong wind or one wrong step is all it takes to tip you right over the edge. But you would be secure if there were appropriate signage and safety features in place.

Who of you has ever read through each of the commandments? Most of us would only really know 2 or 3 of them, just as I did. Some of these I have already mentioned here or there in other chapters as examples. With this in mind, let us have a look at all of the Ten Commandments, complete in their original version, extracted from Exodus 20:3-4, 7-8, 12-17 (NIV), which were presented to Moses roughly 3500 years ago. You can also look them up in Deuteronomy 5:7-21.

I have expanded on each of the verses with some comments in italic letters. Most important though is to understand *why* God protects us from sins:

1. "You shall have no other gods before me."

Because there is only one God, other gods do not exist. God is the source of all life and we are to turn our faces only towards Him. Without God, there is no eternal life. If we follow anything or anyone else, it will not take us to the promised Garden of Eden in God's Kingdom. We will end up on the opposite side, the dark side. God does not want us to waste our time.

2. "You shall not make for yourself an image in the form of anything in heaven above or on the Earth beneath or in the waters below."

The first meaning is obvious, we are not to worship man made objects or hold anything higher than God. Idolatry also refers to placing earthly things ahead of God and so losing our purpose in life. We get tempted to idolise wealth, fame and power and that too is considered a form of idolatry. We only think of the here and now and are tempted to believe that this is it. Instead, we ought to pay attention to each other and on our spiritual development. Chapter "What do I pack for my journey home" expands further on this commandment. Do not waste your precious life on things that don't matter. All idols and statues are only man made. How can a wooden icon or figurine on your mantelpiece possibly help you?

Do not turn away after useless idols. They can do you no good, nor can they rescue you, because they are useless.
1 Samuel 12:21 (NIV)

3. "You shall not misuse the name of the LORD your God, for the LORD will not hold anyone guiltless who misuses his name."

God is the Highest Being that exists. How can we have but the upmost respect and love for Him. People these days use God's name to curse. Worst of all is that it has become part of the vocabulary. Are people really aware of what they are saying? Following verses point out the severity of ignoring this commandment:

And so I tell you, every kind of sin and slander can be forgiven, but blasphemy against the Spirit will not be forgiven.
Matthew 12:31 (NIV)

28 Truly I tell you, people can be forgiven all their sins and every slander they utter,

*29 but whoever blasphemes against the Holy Spirit will never
be forgiven; they are guilty of an eternal sin."
Mark 3:28-29 (NIV)*

The misuse of the LORD's name can also be in form of a deed,
such as proclaiming to prophesy a message from God, when
in fact it is not. Others pretend to act in the name of God for
their own advantage.

4. "Remember the Sabbath day by keeping it holy."

*As I grew up in a catholic family, we would never do any work
on Sundays. At 18 I lived in England as an Au-pair. I also had
to do household chores on Sundays. I remember how wrong it
felt and how I struggled for the first few months. Eventually
though I got used to it.*

*I continued on when I arrived in Australia. On Sundays,
just like everyone else, I used to cut my grass, vacuum clean
the house, do the laundry or anything else that needed to be
done. At the time, I was not even aware that it went against
one of the Ten Commandments. A couple of years ago I
studied them with my lifegroup. That led me to the decision
never to indulge in any laborious work on Sundays again. It is
only a matter of good time management.*

*When God created Earth, he rested on the seventh day.
According to His own example, He gave us this command so
that we too can get a rest. It gives us the space to spend
quality time with our family and friends, relax and devote some
of this time to God. We get a chance to replenish our energy
reserves.*

*It only takes one look at the state of people these days.
Most of them are stressed out, over tired and overworked
which brings about premature death and sicknesses. I guess
our Creator knows what our physical bodies need. We are not
designed to work without a rest, just as flowers don't bloom
continuously.*

5. "Honour your father and your mother, so that you may live long in the land the Lord your God is giving you."

Respect for your parents, others and God. As Children we first learn how to respect our parents and listen to them. We have to follow their rules as they know better and have the experience. Later on as we expand our terrain, we extend what we have learned to our friends, work colleagues and people we meet along the way. The love and respect of our parents is the steppingstone to a relationship with God as we learn and grow to love Him.

6. "You shall not murder."

This is quite straightforward. Most of us can tick that one off…I hope… Another way of looking at it is if we all belong together, interconnected as one, how then can we kill a part of us? Can you cut off your own arm? Jesus took this further and stressed that if we have any quarrels or misunderstandings with one another to sort out the differences without any delay. You can find it in Matthew 5:21-26.

Murder does not necessarily relate to 'killing' a person. One can also 'kill' a person psychologically by breaking their spirit with continuous verbal abuse. We need to take great care of how and what we talk with each other.

7. "You shall not commit adultery."

This is also a commandment that we all understand very well. But in reality, how many of us can tick this one off? No affair has ever had a happy ending. Too many people get hurt and families get destroyed. Children have to endure so much anguish growing up in broken homes. It is not a very good example to learn from at such an early age. They don't even get a chance to experience how a healthy family dynamic ought to function. "For what we were, they are today." *Is this what we want to pass on to our kids? It results in serious consequences that will affect generations to come. Is it worth it?*

The Bible even states that just a thought or a lustful look is a sin. Pretty scary. But all things start with a thought. A very good example is the story of King David, which you can find in the OT (2 Samuel 11 verse 1 onwards)

This is what the LORD Almighty says: "Give careful thought to your ways.
Haggai 1:7 (NIV)

It is also mentioned in 1:5

For it is from within, out of a person's heart, that evil thoughts come—sexual immorality, theft, murder,
Mark 7:21 (NIV)

8. "You shall not steal."

This is another Commandment that ought to make sense, or does it? First thing we think of is shoplifting or stealing from a person. But there are many other kinds of thefts: intellectual theft such as downloading pirate copies of movies and music or steeling other people's intellectual property. Who has never done that? I too have to put my hand up. The Internet gives us plenty of opportunities. In the corporate world, businesses claim that the loss from theft of goods and merchandise doesn't rank as high as time theft by staff; it costs them a tremendous amount of money. People make excuses and believe that these companies are so big and won't notice anyway. It is all about the principle, be honest even in times of great temptation. All big things start small; one thing leads to another. We could add many other kinds of thefts to this list.

Worst of all is that theft not only refers to items but also to human trafficking. People are still beings taken against their will or kidnapped. They are sold off for exploitation, slavery, underage marriage and prostitution. In most cases, they are only children.

9. "You shall not give false testimony against your neighbour."

Do not lie. Every liar will eventually get tangled up in their lies, regardless whether you lie to others or to yourself. What use is lying in the first place? When you lie, whom do you actually lie to? The end effect is that we lie to God. Lies never bring any luck. They only make situations worse. Eventually one will stumble over the lies. Better to take the plunge and face the music straight up. A clean slate makes life much more enjoyable. Lies only wrap chains around us, creating a heavy burden of guilt that drags us down even deeper.

10. "You shall not covet your neighbour's house. You shall not covet your neighbour's wife, or his male or female servant, his ox or donkey, or anything that belongs to your neighbour."

Covet: verb; yearn to possess or have (something).

The grass always seems greener on the other side. God knows that and He doesn't want us to fall into this trap. To desire someone else's possession or status only leads to envy and jealousy. As the Bible tells us, do not compare yourself with others. We will explore this further in chapter 'God given Gifts and Talents'.

Taking a closer look at the Commandments, the wording could come straight out of any self-development book; only, the Bible came first! Could it be that perhaps all these self-help books were just copied? We have all these philosophers, motivational speakers, life style gurus and so forth who believe that they invented the original *what to do's* and *what not to do's* to achieve a happy, successful, healthy and fulfilling life. However, this wisdom has already been around for thousands of years, actually, since the beginning of time (see Genesis…)

It is very simple, all we have to do is make a commitment

and avoid all temptations and overcome our human weaknesses. Very easy to say, but in reality, can we actually do it and stick with it? Of course not. No one is, nor can anyone ever be perfect other than God. This is exactly why we need God in our life. With God on our side, we become stronger, able to break free of the wrong desires and selfish ambitions and turn towards values that really matter. When we happen to trip over, and we will, God will help us back on our feet as often as it takes.

If we continue to do life on our own, it is just going to be like any other New Year's resolution, made with absolute sincerity, only to be broken a short while after. Slowly our good intentions convert to tedious chores. How many of us have planned to visit the gym three times a week and then eventually let the membership expire? Our daily walk can become a bit too tiresome, whereas watching a movie on our cosy lounge suite sounds much more attractive, especially on a cold and rainy day. Moreover, what happened to this diet plan of ours that we started with such enthusiasm? The chocolates and lollies are just too tempting. As a result we remain unfit, eat unhealthy foods, feel horrible about ourselves and eventually guilt becomes a constant companion.

Which points right back to the core of the apple…God, whose perfect ways lead to eternal life

Why not sin?

It all began in the Garden of Eden. Making use of the God-given free will, Eve ignored God's instructions and gave in to the temptation to eat the forbidden fruit (it wasn't an apple by the way). Up to this moment, their souls were pure and one with God, but that all changed from this point on. Since then we are all sinners. What does this mean? Are we all bad people? Did God really create 'bad' people?

It is a very difficult topic to come to terms with. It is much easier to brush it aside rather than attempt to figure out what it portends. We are all born innocent, but the soul is blemished by an imbedded inclination to do things our own way. These 'things' are called sin and prevent us from connecting with the ultimate purity, perfection and life of all life, GOD. He is the source of all there was, is and will be.

13 When tempted, no one should say, "God is tempting me."
For God cannot be tempted by evil, nor does he tempt anyone;
14 but each person is tempted when they are dragged away by their own evil desire and enticed.
James 1:13-14 (NIV)

In the beginning, the connection between God and us was a constant two-way exchange. Energy would flow from either side, from God to us and vice versa. Nothing stood in between until the first sin occurred. From then on, the energy would only be flowing <u>from</u> God to us. Humankind was no longer directly linked to God until Jesus came to re-establish a pathway (see chapter 'Stargate JC') for us to connect directly with God.

Apart from the Ten Commandments, God also passed on the Levitical laws to Moses that go into great detail. If you like to look them up, go to Leviticus, chapter 20 under '*Various*

Laws'. Most of them have been set in place for hygiene purposes that prevented contamination and epidemic outbreaks. In those days there was no refrigeration to preserve food nor was there any pharmaceuticals or technology. Other laws are defined for the preservation of human life. It gave people guidelines how to survive and increase in numbers according to our design. The principles and standards of these laws are still applicable today.

- Clean and unclean foods
- Purification after childbirth
- Regulations for defiling skin diseases
- Unlawful sexual relations
- How to treat foreigners
- Respect for parents
- Harvest of the land
- Livestock and agriculture
- Honest business culture
- Prevention of outbreaks of diseases
- Peace and fairness to all
- Maintain social order
- Provision for the elderly, sick and poor

In the New Testament Jesus tells us again how to lead an upright life. We can find the passages in the book of Matthew, from 5:1 to 7:23 (the Sermon of the Mount). Jesus verifies that the laws have not changed:

17 "Do not think that I have come to abolish the Law or the Prophets; I have not come to abolish them but to fulfill them. 18 For truly I tell you, until heaven and Earth disappear, not the smallest letter, not the least stroke of a pen, will by any means disappear from the Law until everything is accomplished.
Matthew 5:17-18 (NIV)

What has changed is that animal sacrifices are no longer required. Sins are now forgiven through Jesus, our intercessor. Here are some of the points that Jesus reiterates on:

• To forgive others as God forgives you

• Settle conflicts instead of allowing them to fester

• Not to murder also means not to have quarrels with your fellowman which is also subject to judgment

• Not to commit adultery also refers to the thoughts as they always lead to actions

• Not to go after revenge; Eye for an eye is not the way to live

• Love your enemy, pray for them and don't be angry and resentful

• Don't brag about your good deeds, what you give to charity, your prayers or fasting, this is between God and you

• There are only two choices; you cannot serve two masters

• Set your emphasis on God rather than worrying about tomorrow (chapter 'Ask and you shalt receive')

• Not to pass judgment on others, leave it to God. We all make mistakes

• Build your house (life) on the rock (Jesus), not on sand (worldly stuff) that does not last

Does this bring us closer to the answer to why we ought not to sin? In other words, should we begin to adhere to what God conveys to us in the Holy Scriptures? Alternatively, can we allow ourselves to continue in our own ways?

What is it that stops us from choosing the right way? Could it be that we are self conscious of other people's opinion? Does it seem impossible to apply the teachings of Jesus to the corporate world? When trying to fit in with the rest of society, we tend to mask who we really are. One often goes along with everyone else just to avoid any possible embarrassment. Either we subject ourselves to peer pressure or we face the dilemma of being ridiculed for being 'different'. By trying to fit in with the rest of the world, we compromise our own integrity. God's ways are not the easy ways. Jesus often refers to what it means to follow him:

13 "Enter through the narrow gate. For wide is the gate and broad is the road that leads to destruction, and many enter through it.
14 But small is the gate and narrow the road that leads to life, and only a few find it.
Mat 7:13-14 (NIV)

However, when you look at it through God's lens, who then is to be classified as 'different'? Is it you or the others around you? Your faith gives you the strength and courage to **stand out** instead of **stand down**. Dare to be different with God's Grace! In God, you will find solace and refuge.

Alternatively, would you really jump off a bridge just because everyone else does? If we live by God's ways, we live in this world but are not of this world. Our world and standards are that of God. He is the only One we are answerable to.

On several occasions, I have referred to the unstable state of our planet. At present, the world seems to be in uproar. In every corner of the Globe we find turmoil, caused by wars, conflicts or natural disaster. It is becoming a real challenge to switch on the news and be bombarded with horrific stories of utter devastation and despair.

Could this be the result of how we have distanced ourselves further from God? Even our laws are starting to deviate from God's laws. Are we beginning to experience the repercussions/punishment? Are we starting to wear the consequences of our past behaviour? All the decisions we make today will affect the future of our children. Do we have the right to conduct ourselves so negligently that will destroy a good future for our children? They are so innocent and have no choice but to continue from where we will have left off. It all comes back to our short term versus long term view.

I don't wish to go into any specific areas for a reason. This book is only meant to bring forth a contemplative mindset that is able to project a view that reaches far beyond the generations yet to walk on this planet.

The book of Proverbs is another resource that offers a multitude of wisdom, applicable to our daily life. It is worth reading and perhaps even pin up some verses at home or at your office. A good example is gossip, which is one of the forbidden fruit:

Without wood a fire goes out; without a gossip a quarrel dies down.
Proverbs 26:20 (NIV)

Every fight leads to pain and hurt, with a no-win situation. One may win the battle, but no one wins the war. Everyone ends up as a loser. When you gossip about someone, you may think you are in the right. But all you do is create negative energies that affect both, the other person AND YOU! Neither will an argument ever resolve an issue. This is why Jesus said: Love your enemy:

But I tell you, love your enemies and pray for those who persecute you,
Matthew 5:44 (NIV)

So, when you are ready to walk alongside with God, ask Him for help. He is the one who gives you the strength to combat temptations. You cannot do it on your own, nor were you ever meant to. There is no compromise; by living outside these laws, our souls remain tarnished and cannot become one with God. Can you mix oil with water? God's laws are the blueprints that lead to eternal life in His Kingdom.

Another picture would be that of a staircase which leads to eternal life. Each of the Commandments represents one step. If we were to remove only one of the steps, the whole staircase would collapse, leaving us stranded.

As I was journeying through the BiOY programme in 2014, I realised that all the laws are based on the two laws that Jesus tells us:

*37 Jesus replied: "**Love the Lord your God with all your heart and with all your soul and with all your mind.'**
38 This is the first and greatest commandment.*
Matthew 22:37-39 (NIV)

*39 And the second is like it: '**Love your neighbour as yourself.'**
40 All the Law and the Prophets hang on these two commandments."*
Matthew 22:39-40 (NIV)

You will also find them in the Gospel of Mark 12:29-31. If we were to adhere to these two, how could we possibly break any of the other commandments?

At first they both made sense to me, but after deliberating on the second one a bit deeper, I started to get confused. Is it possible that Jesus made a mistake? How can one possibly love a neighbour if one cannot even love oneself? Who loves themselves? I do now, but it took me many years. There is so much self-hate due to low self-esteem brought on by how others judge us. Careless, envious or cruel remarks make us believe that we don't measure up to certain standards. They lead us to believe that we don't look good enough or are not smart enough. People are slow in seeing the good in others; instead, they focus on what is wrong. By judging the book by its cover, the content never gets to be appreciated.

Then again, Jesus is perfect and never made a single mistake. He had the correct answer to every question, no matter how complex they were. The Pharisees often tried to get Jesus to trip up with 'trick' questions and never succeeded. So my question to God was: how can someone love others if they hate themselves? Would these people then be exempt from this Commandment? For a long time my logical mind could not grasp the concept of loving others whilst lacking self love. Finally, I realised what prevented me from seeing its logic. I had applied my mind instead of my heart to find the answer. Then, I love these moments; it dawned on me when God gave me the insight. Firstly, there are TWO Commandments, not one. My focus was only on the second one because I understood the first, so I thought. I ignored the important fact that they have been put in this order for a specific reason. To love the 'invisible' God is the hardest but foremost important Commandment. Love God every day, learn to nurture love in your heart constantly. Then you can begin to learn to love who you are and transfer this love to others around you. That is, not only at church or in the company of family and friends, but also to your adversaries. It has to be consistent and without any favouritism. At that point, when you realise this, you will be able to experience God's unconditional love and greatness. This completes the circle of love. How can you but love yourself? But we humans tend to slack off and fall back into our old habits. The following quote speaks perfectly into this space:

"I really only love God as much as I love the person I love the least."
- Dorothy Day -

Next time you come across a person that you don't particular like, ask yourself: Do I really love God? How then is it that I dislike this person? By disapproving of others, I also disapprove of God; because in every human being exists a part of God. As individuals we all form a part of an organic existence. There is much more to life than chasing after the impossible. We always have to keep in mind that every thought, word and action affects someone or something.

If the heart misses only one beat, there are consequences; we can lose consciousness, have a stroke or may even die. One wrong word or deed can have a devastating effect on others around us. It can destroy a person's or even your own life. Words have caused many wars.

Not just external and physical matters are connected; also our spiritual being is intertwined with the whole of Creation. Jesus tells us how we should live our life in accordance to God's Commandments, which He followed to the letter. The Commandments express how we need to fit into the entire spectrum of Creation, physically and spiritually.

Regrettably, the only living thing that does not tend to 'function' very well is the human being, the pinnacle of God's Creation; the icing on the cake, the one to which He has given the free will to make its own choices. Only, the icing has gone off a tad whilst the rest of the 'cake' is slowly being affected. The perfect harmony is being compromised. We need to start to behave ourselves as part of an undivided Creation.

"God's Laws - the template to a fulfilling life with the promise of eternal existence"
- Monica -

I believe this life is meant for recognising and breaking down the barriers that stand between God and us. These barriers are called sins. With the God given free will, we have also been given the responsibility to make our own choices. They either will see us re-united with God or separated from Him. In essence, we can only re-enter God's domain if we can 'lift' ourselves to His frequency/vibration. To make this possible, He has sent Jesus to shepherd us (Chapter "Who is Jesus").

The purpose of our life is also to help and support others on their journey. No matter how we phrase it, we always end up with the same conclusion. You would have noticed the common pattern in each of the chapters. It all leads back to God who is the core of everything, the Alpha and Omega, the beginning and the end, the ever-living uncreated Creator.

God - Love - Life - Light - Truth

And He wants us all to join Him at the 'heavenly' banquet. There cannot be anything more desirable than dwell in a dimension where everything is perfect. Like lost children, we have to find our way back to God. God is the truth. As it is written:

Jesus answered, "I am the way and the truth and the life
John 14:6 (NIV)

When Jesus spoke again to the people, he said, "I am the light of the world. Whoever follows me will never walk in darkness, but will have the light of life."
John 8:12 (NIV)

In the beginning of this chapter, I touched on the implications of our choices and what consequences they will have. In the Old Testament God refers to them as punishment:

Deuteronomy 23.2 (NIV):
2 No one born of a forbidden marriage nor any of their descendants may enter the assembly of the LORD, not even in the tenth generation.

Numbers 14:18 (or exodus 34:7) (NIV)
18'The LORD is slow to anger, abounding in love and forgiving sin and rebellion. Yet he does not leave the guilty unpunished; he punishes the children for the sin of the parents to the third and fourth generation.'

Deuteronomy 5:9 (or Exodus 20:5) (NIV):
9 You shall not bow down to them or worship them; for I, the LORD your God, am a jealous God, punishing the children for the sin of the parents to the third and fourth generation of those who hate me,

But followed by Deuteronomy 5:10 (or Exodus 20:6) (NIV)

10 but showing love to a thousand generations of those who love me and keep my commandments.

What really stands out is that the reward by far outweighs the punishment. Up to ten generations have to endure the consequences but thousands of generations are being blessed for keeping God's ways. It really means forever. It gives us a glimpse of what is yet to come, the promise of God.

5 For the LORD is good and his love endures forever;
his faithfulness continues through all generations.
Psalm 100:5 (NIV)

In the New Testament the apostle Paul writes in his letter to the Galatians church (and us) to stay clear of a self-centered and inconsiderate way of life:

19 The acts of the flesh are obvious: sexual immorality, impurity and debauchery;
20 idolatry and witchcraft; hatred, discord, jealousy, fits of rage, selfish ambition, dissensions, factions
21 and envy; drunkenness, orgies, and the like. I warn you, as I did before, that those who live like this will not inherit the kingdom of God.
Galatians 5:19-21 (NIV)

These characteristics have serious repercussions. These days many of them are not even being considered as bad or offensive. Society is slowly being shaped to fit in with such behaviours through the media, movies, games and Internet. The community has grown indifferent and gradually started to accept this as the 'norm'. Worst of all, our children are exposed to such ugliness at a too young an age. Where is all this leading? What values will the next generation be able to pass on to their descendants? Is this what God warns us of? So many things we do today appear innocent or acceptable, but are they really?

How will this affect the future of humankind and its existence?

At present, we get the impression that the world is governed by evil. The world is in turmoil, tormented by an increasing amount of natural disasters taking thousands of lives and fanatical wars killing millions of innocent people. God allows us to choose our own final destiny. But you can rest assured; in the end love will prevail. When the time comes, God will shun all evil and give birth to a new life, a kind of life that we cannot possibly imagine. Who knows, maybe there will be a third book added to the Holy Bible:

The Old Testament
The New Testament
The *Ultimate Testament*... (just a thought)

18 We know that anyone born of God does not continue to sin; the One who was born of God keeps them safe, and the evil one cannot harm them.
19 We know that we are children of God, and that the whole world is under the control of the evil one.
1 John 5:18-19 (NIV)

On the upside, let us conclude this chapter with good news. God has given us His greatest gift, the gift of His Holy Spirit and by His Spirit we can change:

22 But the fruit of the Spirit is love, joy, peace, forbearance, kindness, goodness, faithfulness,
23 gentleness and self-control. Against such things there is no law.
Galatians 5:22 (NIV)

and:

The fruit of the righteous is a tree of life.
and the one who is wise saves lives.
Proverbs 11:30 (NIV)

Through our sins the empire of darkness grows, however, our righteousness and love for God will conquer all evil:

Let your light shine bright and strong
Nourished with the love of Jesus
Never let your fire grow weak
but let your good work prevail

Let your light shine bright and strong
All of you, link your hands
Together stand firm against the darkness
And proclaim that God is your LORD

Let your light shine bright and strong
Cast away the thoughts of shadows
That there will be no darkness
for the evil one to hide

Let your light shine bright and strong
For we can rest assured
that Love will claim the final victory
in the name of our Lord Jesus Christ

Monica

Which points right back to the core of the apple…God, who holds the sword of victory

Why God's Ways?

Who is in Control?

16 Your eyes saw my unformed body;
all the days ordained for me were written in your
book
before one of them came to be.
17 How precious to me are your thoughts, God!
How vast is the sum of them!

Psalm 139:16-17 (NIV)

...

The secret things belong to the Lord our God,
but the things revealed belong to us and to our
children forever,
that we may follow all the words of this law.

Deuteronomy 29:29 (NIV)

Without trust, one is incapable to let go of control. The verses in Psalm 139 tell us that God knows each one of us before we are born. He knows exactly what lies ahead for us. The plan has been drawn up long before the beginning.

We need to put our trust in God and His perfect plan, even at times when we cannot make sense of what is happening around us. If we were to replace our doubts with trust and allow God at the helm, life would no longer be a labyrinth with countless dead-ends.

A Pound of Bread

I have a wonderful childhood memory that I would like to share with you. It renders a perfect picture of what trust is:

During the time I grew up, the world was still a safe place and parents were able to let their children walk to and from school or send them out on little errands.

Occasionally my mother would ask us to go across the road to get a couple of little things she needed from the local grocer. She would hand me a little purse with change and send me on my way. I remember that she told me the exact words to say when I got to the shop. I was then going to kinder and didn't understand all the words the 'big' people were using, especially not what mum was telling me: 'A pound of bread'.

All the way to the grocer I would rehearse the words over and over in my head so as not to forget them. It was like heading off to an exam. I was so worried that I may forget by the time I got to the shop. So when I reached the shop, I very quickly gushed out the words just like my mum told me. It was more like blurting out some syllables that made sense to everybody except me. I had no idea what I was saying, but trusted my mum that if I did and said exactly what she instructed me, the girl at the counter would know what to do. Then I could just pass my purse over to her, grab my shopping and run home. I couldn't wait to get back to the world that I understood and felt safe in.

Doesn't this story draw a wonderful parallel to what God

means by trusting Him? Should we not just follow His instructions, even if we don't understand? If we were to trust in His guidance without questions and doubts, what sort of life could we lead? If we were to 'blurt out' with the trust and innocence of a child, would it not turn out perfectly too? Instead, people spend so much time complaining how badly life is treating them; suffer from disappointments or feeling lost and helpless in difficult and trying times. Oblivious to the fact that help is so very near, people still choose to go ahead and plough through life whilst facing the ramifications of failures and regrets.

Depression is so widely spread these days. It is as easy as to get a GP to write out a prescription for antidepressants. Therefore the cause of depression is not necessarily established and treated. People miss out on finding a less intrusive course of treatment. Consequently we have psychiatrists, psychologists and counselors who are making a fortune treating people with depression, addictions or other psychological conditions.

Searching for the true reason is not easy. People find it too confronting to be honest with themselves and take time out to evaluate their situation. Alas, loneliness is the most common predicament that people are facing today. The new era of 'cyberspace living' is a breeding ground for loneliness and depression. For so many it becomes inevitable. Online communications deprive people from physical interaction and human touch. This is an elementary human need. Our make-up demands a life shared in community with others. Relationships and friendships are meant to be personal not virtual.

By glaring into a TV screen or getting caught up in computer games, one does not notice that life is passing by like a fast train. We are meant to be in it for the ride, not standing by on the sidelines, watching it race past us. Yes indeed, it does take some courage to jump on board of a train with destination 'Unknown'. All it takes is to trust that the driver will take us safely to our designated station.

Everyone is in search of his or her 'Garden of Eden' on their own, therefore never quite finding it. Eventually people can no longer endure the emptiness inside and slowly 'burn out'. They continuously feel unfulfilled and try to numb the pain of failure and regrets with addictions such as drugs, alcohol, gambling, eating, sex, pornography, TV, shopping, computer or internet games, violence and the list goes on. The void persists and they lose their grip on reality as they estrange themselves further and further away from the true essence of their existence. They live in an artificial matrix. These people are unaware of the fact that their superficial activities only prohibit them from searching for answers and resolve the cause of the issues.

We all board the same cruise ship
We all have the same captain
And we all want to sit at the captain's table
with the promise of a glorious journey
which takes us to the final harbour

Some don't trust the Captain
They disembark to visit other places
places that were not meant to be
Their own choice of direction
will not take them to the final harbour

But others are willing to trust the captain
They choose to stay on board
Enjoying the comfort and security of the ship
knowing that the promises of the captain
will come true at the final harbour

Monica

We are spiritual beings, living in a physical body for only a relatively short time. Our physical body is designed to expire. We are here to make a decision who and what we will ultimately follow and believe which then will determine our final destination.

So who do we trust? Do we just get off the boat and go wherever our own desires take us? Or do we stay on board and invest the wonderful gift of life in a truly meaningful and worthy way? Do we want a joyous or troublesome journey? Life can be a long and lonely road. It is our choice to walk through the maze of life on our own or to recognise that there is a Creator out there who knows the right way. He is the only one who possesses the full view.

As a child I fully trusted and relied on my mother's directions. To get what I was meant to take home, I 'recited' her exact words. So can we, as adults learn how to trust and follow God like a child.

At that time Jesus said, "I praise you, Father, Lord of heaven and Earth, because you have hidden these things from the wise and learned, and revealed them to little children.
Matthew 11:25 (NIV)

And he (Jesus) said: "Truly I tell you, unless you change and become like little children, you will never enter the kingdom of heaven.
Matthew 18:3 (NIV)

Those two verses distinctly point towards the same implications. As adults we can be very stubborn and self-reliant. Often we are too proud to admit that we need help. Therefore we go our own lonely ways and miss out on the promise of a fulfilling and significant life, in companionship with family and friends. The verses also highlight that we need the confidence and the mind of a child. Children still have a fresh approach to all situations, lacking any preconceived ideas and limitations. With unconditional trust they look up to their parents. The mother is always there with food, clothes, nurturing and a warm home; she is the 'save haven' to run home to. The father is the provider and indisputable hero; nothing appears to be impossible for him. He has always something to teach and show you. He keeps the family safe and takes you to sport and maybe even on some adventures.

The brain of every baby does not contain any 'corrupted' thoughts, just like a brand new computer. It is free of negativities and 'viruses'. The moment the child starts growing up it gets exposed to bad viruses: Optimism, joy, confidence and the drive to conquer the big wide world out there is being suppressed by pessimism, negativity and constraints. It was researched that the word YES is by far outweighed by NO. Children from a very young age are bombarded with 'NO', 'YOU CAN'T' or 'DON'T'. Thus, negativity often preempts a positive and healthy environment in which to grow up in.

Be like a child, trust and go forward in life, assured that all things are possible with God, provided that the intentions are just. Stop relying on your own wisdom and strength. Reach out, trust and allow God to take the lead.

> *5 Trust in the LORD with all your heart*
> *and lean not on your own understanding;*
> *6 in all your ways submit to him,*
> *and he will make your paths straight.*
>
> *7 Do not be wise in your own eyes;*
> *fear the LORD and shun evil.*
> *8 This will bring health to your body*
> *and nourishment to your bones.*
> *Proverbs 3:5-8 (NIV)*

Before we continue, I'd like to define the word 'fear'. It is so often misunderstood and taken literally, which I used to do myself. In a church, I once caught sight of a plaque on the wall that said: "*Thou shalt fear the LORD*". I interpreted *fear* as having to be scared of God and I thought that this sign does not do justice to a loving and gentle God. Would God really demand of us to be trembling in fear of Him?

When I first started to meet with the lifegroup, we came

across verses that spoke of 'The Fear of the LORD'. I soon learned that the word *fear* stands for the highest and deepest *respect* for God. Fear also tells us how vital it is to accept God without a grain of doubt and with trust, as solid and unmovable as a rock. Engrave your faith and trust firmly in your heart. You will experience the same as you did with your parents; being unconditionally loved, provided and cared for and feeling absolutely safe and protected. Then God will reveal His wisdom to you that assists you to master any obstacles that you encounter in your life.

In the very beginning of His ministry, Jesus would teach in a word by word fashion, but then, soon after, He only spoke in parables. Often it can be very difficult to understand. Some of the meanings can be interpreted in different ways. Still, they all convey the wisdom of God. Wouldn't it be much easier if it were written in a straightforward text? This is exactly how I felt when I first took up reading the Bible. Some parables didn't quite make sense to me and others made perfect sense.

Here is an example of a personal experience:

In my first lifegroup, our leader was asking if each of us would like to prepare and lead a session. It was a terrific idea and we were very excited to get ourselves engaged in finding an interesting topic that we could discuss. My initial idea was to address the miracles of healing that Jesus performed which had always fascinated me. My favourite one is when Jesus said to the paralysed man, "Get up, take your mat and go home". Anything is possible by the power of God.

Anyhow, as I started to look for some verses I had a change of plans. Some of you may not know yet that various Bibles indicate everything spoken by Jesus in red letters. I felt drawn towards taking the group through some of the 'red letter' verses instead. What could be more revealing and true than what Jesus Himself is saying? So I searched for the 'red letters' and selected some parables. I picked the ones that I understood and made commentary notes for the discussions.

On the night when it was my turn, I grabbed my worksheets and with great enthusiasm, made my way to the meeting. I was looking forward towards stimulating discussions. However, my plans did not line up with what God intended to teach us. I believe we only got to read one verse for the whole evening. Totally unaware, I managed, with God's help, to open a can of worms. We ended up discussing the purpose of the parables. It all turned out different to what I had expected but with an incredibly interesting outcome. We learned a lot that night. It went well, even without any prepared notes. God knew we didn't require any. What we found were the following verses that explain why Jesus, in most cases made use of parables:

> *9 His disciples asked him what this parable meant.*
> *10 He (Jesus) said, "The knowledge of the secrets of the kingdom of God has been given to you, but to others I speak in parables, so that,*
> *" 'though seeing, they may not see;*
> *though hearing, they may not understand.'*
> *Luke 8:9-10 (NIV)*

I experienced the same encounter whilst reading the Bible. You will only ever be able to understand what God wants you to. The same applies to Jesus's parables. Whoever God has chosen will understand, but the ones that don't believe are left out. Ultimately, God is in control, even if some are convinced that they don't need God and keep everything under their own rule. People, who believe in the superiority and sovereignty of God, allow themselves to be led. They have no desire to take over. They know that God has the best interest at heart for anyone who follows Him. At church as well as at lifegroup gatherings, we always open with a prayer. We invite the presence of God and ask that the Holy Spirit would lead and teach us.

I couldn't resist quoting the upcoming verses as it reminds me of an experience I had not so long ago, the famous scene of Jesus walking on water. It has even been an inspiration for many movies. Could this be the next thing humans try to accomplish?

47 Later that night, the boat was in the middle of the lake, and he (Jesus) was alone on land.
48 He saw the disciples straining at the oars, because the wind was against them. Shortly before dawn he went out to them, walking on the lake. He was about to pass by them,
49 but when they saw him walking on the lake, they thought he was a ghost. They cried out,
50 because they all saw him and were terrified. Immediately he spoke to them and said, "Take courage! It is I. Don't be afraid."
51 Then he climbed into the boat with them, and the wind died down.
Mark 6:47-51 (NIV)

However, do people actually understand the heart of the message? It was not really meant to prove that Jesus could walk on water. That would have been the equivalent to a 'walk in the park' for Jesus. Jesus was teaching His apostles by the means of an action. He is telling us that in any situation, we are not alone; God is always around us and helps us to calm the storms of our lives. With faith in God, we are capable of anything.

We encountered horrendous storms in Melbourne that caused real havoc. Big trees were uprooted; fences blown over and damage to many properties were reported:

During the night when the storm was at its worst, I was woken up by a howling wind. It gave me an uneasy feeling. First thing I did was check on how my dog, which sleeps on my bed, was reacting. Animals with their primary instinct always know if there is any real danger. To my surprise he was perked up and that got me so scared. I could feel how fear was starting to rise up on the inside. I knew that if I wasn't going to do anything and continued to churn over in my mind how scared I was, I would end up in a real panic. I was close to losing my calm, imagining all sorts of things that could happen.

Tears even started to come up. In an effort to get back in control, I told myself that I was responsible and had to be the "strong leader" here. I needed to get a grip on myself quick smart. So I got up and started wandering around the house, talking aloud to my dog. I told him that all is well and under control (I almost believed it myself). Just to keep myself occupied, I closed all the door doors, and then went back to bed. The wind kept on howling and I was still feeling panicky. Nothing had changed to make me feel any better. Then, finally, I remembered God! I started to pray and envisioned the story in which Jesus was in a boat with his disciples during a big storm:

23 Then he got into the boat and his disciples followed him.
24 Suddenly a furious storm came up on the lake, so that the waves swept over the boat. But Jesus was sleeping.
25 The disciples went and woke him, saying, "LORD, save us! We're going to drown!"
26 He replied, "You of little faith, why are you so afraid?" Then he got up and rebuked the winds and the waves, and it was completely calm.
27 The men were amazed and asked, "What kind of man is this? Even the winds and the waves obey him!"
Matthew 8:23-27 (NIV)

Yes, what kind of God is He I said to myself. He is the One who created everything; therefore He can calm any storm, even this one. I continued to pray and hung on to the picture of Jesus, standing in the boat and calming the wind. It was like a mantra: "Please God, calm the storm, I know you can. Just stretch out your mighty arm and the winds will cease. Send the wind away somewhere where it cannot do any harm to anyone. Please God, make it go away, please calm the storm."

Every so often I would stop and listen out for any changes. Slowly I began to feel better. After a while I couldn't hear the wind howling so violently anymore and was able to fall back to sleep. I was under the impression that the wind had calmed down.

The next day though, people at work told me that it went on all night. I could hardly believe it. God had calmed my inner storm and kept me safe so that I was able to sleep peacefully.

As for God, his way is perfect:
The LORD's word is flawless;
he shields all who take refuge in him.
Psalm 18:30 (NIV)

My prayer:

LORD Jesus,
I pray for all the readers that they would ask you to come on board too.
May they, from here on, journey through life with You at their side.
I ask that you would stretch out your strong and mighty arm over them and protect them.
Please replace all fear from their hearts with joy and give them the freedom to be who You have created them to be.
Thank you Jesus

Amen

Which points right back to the core of the apple…God, our Father who gives us joy and protection

God's View

God has given us a free will. Therefore He will never force us to do anything we don't want to do. He prompts us by sending us His words through feelings, dreams, friends, books, events, movies, magazines and above all for the ones who believe in His book, the Bible. His words are meant for all of us.

It all depends how much attention we pay to what is going on around us. Are your eyes and ears open? Do you consciously observe the world around you? Or are you going too fast and miss the signs?

God is our catalyst. He gives us ownership of what we do, the good as well as the bad. Ultimately we are responsible for our own decisions and actions. When we draw closer to God, we learn how to view the world from His perspective. We begin to understand the meaning and purpose of life with more clarity. We learn and begin to think and act in a 'Christlike' way.

> For my thoughts are not your thoughts,
> neither are your ways my ways,"
> declares the LORD.
> Isaiah 55:8 (NIV)

When we do life on our own, we only pay attention to the world that is visible. But once we acknowledge the existence of God, our thinking will slowly transform. We begin to look through Gods eyes and the world around us changes significantly.

What we thought we couldn't live without moves out of focus and becomes irrelevant. What used to be so important fades and gives way to things that we never even considered. We start to look at other human beings through loving eyes. There are times I could hug a person on sheer impulse, but it is not always appropriate to do so of course. The more love you send out the more you will yield. People can sense that you mean well and respond in kindness. I try to keep myself from criticising and instead focus on finding out who this person really is. It is very difficult and often I fall back into my old habits of criticising and judging others. Through whose eyes do you want to form your view on life and your own part in it? Which lens projects the true picture?

It was only about a year ago when I took my aunty and uncle to the Eureka Building. They were visiting from overseas and had never been in a skyscraper. When we reached the 88th floor, we were dazzled by a spectacular view. I was observing people walking and running, cars navigating through traffic, trains pulling out of the station, heading off into the distance, trams and buses picking up passengers and taxis lined up waiting for a fare.

This outing inspired me with a colourful analogy that draws a likely picture of how God would feel when He looks upon us: blindly "stumbling" through life and ignoring His wisdom and guidance:

Imagine yourself standing on the top floor (88th) of the Eureka building in Melbourne. This is pretty high. You can see all around you and far into the distance. You can make out ships, cars, trains, trams, bikes and people moving like little toys. It looks somewhat cute and at the same time unreal. You feel like someone watching a puppet show and as if you could almost reach out to set the scene in a different way.

Wow, over there, this guy could have turned left to avoid an upcoming traffic jam caused by road works. Only he couldn't see it. Down there in the park, a mother is frantically looking for her child. It is hiding behind a bush. You wish you could move the bush away to put the mother's mind at peace. Only from above can one have a complete perspective. It is so much fun observing the world from up there; safe and with the best view ever, nothing gets unnoticed.

But then, just as you turn around, still a smile on your face, you see an enormous cloud approaching. All of a sudden you realise that this is a huge sand storm blowing over from the desert, due to cause devastation in only a few moments. Your immediate thought is to warn everyone and you hurriedly reach for your phone and call 000. To your utter surprise, the operator does not seem to take it seriously and is not listening to what you are saying.

Despite your warnings, nothing was undertaken to warn the public and the storm approaches rapidly. In total disbelief and helplessness, you watch the scenario unfold right in front of you. There is nothing in your power to change its course.

How does God feel when He guides people from even *greater heights?* A view from a spaceship cannot even compare to the view that God has. He can see beyond all. His view is not limited to timelines; the past, present and future. He knows the beginning before it begins. He knows the outcome even before it was planned. His view has no geographical restrictions, neither here on Earth or in the spiritual reality. So, who else is out there that has a better position and possesses eternal wisdom? Who else is capable to lead us the right and only way?

Many are the plans in a person's heart, but it is the LORD's
purpose that prevails.
Proverbs 19:21 (NIV)

We think we are in control, make plans, have visions of where we want to be and in the end, things turn out so differently. At first we tend to be dissatisfied with the outcome, blaming others or ourselves for not having achieved a certain goal, only to realise that it turned out much better than planned; provided that you are lucky enough to change course and choose another route. Some people are stubborn and, failing to recognise that they are not in control, end up with disappointments. Discouraged they turn bitter with deep regrets. Haven't we all asked ourselves this question at one point: "If only I had…?" We cannot turn back time and start all over again. What is left in the end is emptiness with no worthwhile achievements and with only a 'wasted' life to look back to. Regret is far worse than failure. It is by far better to try and fail than never to give it a shot and end up with regrets.

What we need to do is stay tuned with our Creator; stay on the same channel and continue to listen for directions. We cannot see the whole picture from down here, but we have God watching over us. Whoever realises this knows that all will go well by remaining faithful and flexible enough to adapt to new circumstances. We need to change in how and what we think, plan and follow up with the actions which God advises. Just like listening to the traffic report on the radio station on the way to work. Would you continue on your present course if an accident were announced that happened further on? You certainly would seek an alternative route as quickly as possible.

One of the ways we can accomplish this is to stop rushing heedlessly through the days, weeks, months and years. Instead, we should slow down to take a good look around ourselves and become aware of our surroundings. Once the focus is redirected from our own private little world onto others around us, it is surprising how life will change. God has it all planned to perfection. Nothing happens without God's consent. Nothing and no one can slip through the cracks unnoticed.

God's ways are equivalent to railway tracks. They are mapped out on a chart, interlinked with all the other lines. The trains run along their assigned tracks and cannot go the wrong way. They safely negotiate through the complex network of intersecting tracks as the points are being switched from the control centre at the right time. The train stops at all the designated stations. Our paths too have been pre-set. We all have the same destination, the end of the line. But we all board a different train from different places; have different routes with different stations. Some of the stops may not always appear right and we wonder what is going on. Nonetheless as we set off to the next station, we realise it was the right one.

As the saying goes, all roads lead to Rome, however, it is not Rome that we need to focus on. It is the HOW we get there. The journey will inevitably be the key to a life of true purpose.

Each station is a part of our life and it does matter where we stop along the way. God has carefully chosen every station for each individual person. All stations are preselected to lead us to specific experiences, lessons and people we meet. Every circumstance we encounter impacts outcomes of the whole spectrum of Creation and its course. Every station is like a piece of a huge puzzle, blending in with everyone else. The upshot is that whatever may look like an utter mayhem to us will all in the end fit together as one complete and perfect picture.

We are free to choose and change tracks and our direction anytime. Are we equipped to make such decisions without God's input? Do we, as humans, possess the capacity to comprehend the enormous complexity of an all-dimensional existence? How then could there be the smallest hope to even get close to understanding the big plan? Who and what do we influence in our life? If we veer off just a bit, whom else will we affect by our choices?

With faith in the all-knowing eternal God, it is easy to remain on the mutually selected route. In other words, **faith is the railway track on which one can never get lost**. Having that peace of mind and trust within, all of life's challenges can be overcome. The necessary strength, endurance, courage, wisdom and insight will always be available to us at the right moment. Best of all, you know that you are following your designated track. It is unavoidable that every person needs to go through an array of emotions in life, both sides of the spectrum, happy and sad. If there were never any tribulations, how then would we know what happy is? If you don't experience hardship, how could you know what prosperity is? Everything has to have an opposite to balance.

Why not allow God to set the points for your tracks in your life? Another way of looking at it is the use of a GPS. You are on your way to visit friends and have never been there before. Most definitely you will resort to your satellite system because it will take you there.

By all means, many roads lead to Rome. Do we select

the fast one via freeways, the scenic way through suburbs or do we choose the toll ways?

Life will present itself in a multitude of choices. Then again, you can both rush in and make your own decisions or you can 'tune in' and ask for guidance. In the end, we all will arrive at our appointed destination.

A person's steps are directed by the LORD.
How then can anyone understand their own way?
Proverbs 20:24 (NIV)

Do you believe that God is guiding you? Have you ever had a feeling or a prompting to do something? Have you ever been totally convicted that it must have been from God? It has happened to me a few times. Normally it all turns out the way I had envisioned but there were times when it took a different and unexpected turn. This is when doubt starts to creep in. Was the prompting really from God or was it just me thinking it was a great idea? The outcome appeared to be in complete contrast to my expectations and it seemed like it all backfired. Do I hold or do I fold?

A good example of that happened to me a year and a half ago. After the completion of the Kairos course (about mission) I felt that God prompted me to start up a life group for new Christians, especially for people who had just finished Alpha.

During that time I was still meeting with my first lifegroup. All of us in the group were very eager to learn from the Bible. After every meeting I came home charged up and inspired. We were privileged to have a very caring and knowledgeable leader who taught us a lot. Despite all that, I began to feel that I wanted to start a new group as a leader. I kept this to myself for quite a while because I loved our group and was always looking forward to our meetings on Friday nights. Often it got rather late over discussions and just hanging out together, sharing the day to day stuff. It felt comfortable and I didn't want to leave this behind. Then the unexpected happened.

One night our leader sadly informed us that he and his wife needed to invest more time with their growing boys and couldn't go on with leading a lifegroup. As sad as the news may have been, it came at the right time for me to start organising and preparing for a new group. This was clearly God's plan. So, with great enthusiasm I started to find out how to go about it. The church had even made a room available for us to use. I immersed myself in putting together an action plan and suggestions of which Bible study we can embark on.

I spoke to many people who were very interested in joining the life group. I drafted some worksheets and took my time to make sure that we had a successful launch of our new life group. I sent out e-mails to everyone to suggest some dates. I didn't really get any replies so I set the date for our first gathering.

I brought the worksheets with me and was ready to go. Two people turned up. You can imagine how disappointed I was. But knowing in my heart that God wanted me to do this, I thought that by the following week all would fall into place. It never really turned out the way I envisioned. People were not quite willing to commit to come to the gatherings on a regular basis. I started to miss our lifegroup but I kept going. We still got a bit of a start and met up. We also took part in some social activities. We had fun and the guys bonded so well. Deeper friendships were formed. But it was not the outcome that I had anticipated. I couldn't get a 'proper' Bible study going. At first I was very disappointed and couldn't understand why it wasn't working out. This was my personal view and perception, but God did achieve what He had planned all along.

With great joy I observed how much the group had bonded. They caught up at various different times and were supporting each other and reaching out. They became a little family. Then I began to see that the plan had fully succeeded but with a double effect. I got a new lifegroup together.

The lesson I learnt was that when plans don't develop according to your expectations, hang in there and keep going. I knew that God wanted me to do a certain thing and I needed to remind myself that from where I stood, the view was not as clear as God's view. I was aware that I would always get what I needed for the task at hand.

God didn't mean for life to be as complicated as we make it out to be. On the contrary, it only seems 'complicated' when we live without God. People are against God because they are afraid of giving up control. They only believe in things they can logically explain and physically see. So many of us end up chasing after things that, in reality are not meeting our needs. We 'drive' straight into a traffic jam. In the midst of it we try to handle the situation by our own wisdom and strength that eventually will diminish. But God's wisdom and strength is everlasting. He offers it to us freely, all we have to do is ask, trust and follow. We can have as much of it as we want, an unlimited source of energy, strength and counsel.

The words of Psalm 81 were spoken to the Israelites thousands of years ago, but it still applies to us in the here and now. We all are His chosen people, who at times have stubborn hearts and do it our own way:

> 11 "But my people would not listen to me;
> Israel would not submit to me.
> 12 So I gave them over to their stubborn hearts
> to follow their own devices.
>
> 13 "If my people would only listen to me,
> if Israel would only follow my ways,
> 14 how quickly I would subdue their enemies
> and turn my hand against their foes!
> Psalm 81:11-14 (NIV)

Why do people continue to ignore God's words? What if we were to put our ego in our back pocket to allow us to acknowledge God's view and plans for us?

- God's vision for us to find our own purpose and calling in life
- God's vision for us and our world
- God's vision for us to live in total freedom and take delight in all of His Creation, which sustains us with true happiness; living together in peace and love.

It really cannot be repeated often enough how important it is to take God's will seriously and to focus on the bigger picture. The verses from Psalm 33 so distinctly describe that God knows us all intimately. He has specific plans for each of us. Each plan is tailored to our individual personality and capabilities.

8 Let all the Earth fear the LORD;
let all the people of the world revere him.
9 For he spoke, and it came to be;
he commanded, and it stood firm.

10 The LORD foils the plans of the nations;
he thwarts the purposes of the peoples.
11 But the plans of the Lord stand firm forever,
the purposes of his heart through all generations.

12 Blessed is the nation whose God is the LORD,
the people he chose for his inheritance.
13 From heaven the LORD looks down
and sees all mankind;
14 from his dwelling place he watches
all who live on Earth—
15 he who forms the hearts of all,
who considers everything they do.
Psalm 33:8-15 (NIV)

But most people make their own plans on their own accord. Whenever we go our own way and we try to achieve something, it often comes with a lot of struggles and hardship. We are trying to find a way out of a tangle. Each time when we think we have made it, we discover that we have reached yet another dead-end. Or it can feel like we are hitting our head against an invisible wall, not getting anywhere.

Only a small percentage (10%) of people are able to achieve financial success, fame or power, but even then it never seems to be enough. They continue to search for the ultimate happiness. Looking at it from the outside, they appear to live a very successful and accomplished life. But how does it look from behind the scenes? How do they feel about all their achievements? How about the rest of us; don't we relentlessly wait for the one thing we want which is going to make us happy? There is always that one more thing to get until… until what?

We all can hear God, just in different ways. Maybe you have this little voice telling you something or maybe just a strong feeling or prompting. This is how He tries to guide you. He can see the one-way streets way before you can. Looking from above, life is not a jungle and a roadblock is not a hindrance. We can always take another route knowing that life is not meant to be all up to us. God is our GPS. Have you got it switched on?

I can remember many occasions when I came up with what I thought were brilliant ideas. For instance I wanted to import microfibre cleaning cloths when they first came on the market in Europe. My mother told me about them and sent a few over for me to use. I got so excited about it. So on my visit to Switzerland I got in touch with the manufacturer and even purchased quite a few of those cloths to take back to Australia. But what I needed to achieve was to land it in Australia at a very low cost in order to sell it here. Unfortunately the manufacturer wouldn't come to the party and I tried a couple of other avenues. Whichever way I turned, I hit that famous invisible wall. In the end, I left it at that and moved on. I could have lost a lot of money had I proceeded with this idea. Years later, the market was flooded with microfibre products. It now retails at a fraction of what it would have cost me to import them.

Who hasn't felt like that before? It is quite obvious that the idea may have been ok at the time, but it was not where God wanted me to go. In hindsight, God most likely saved me a lot of money and grief.

On another occasion, only four years ago, I felt compelled to explore the idea of becoming a life coach. In this instance, the whole process just unfolded. Where other students struggled, I sailed through easily. I was able to complete my certificate in half the time. I haven't yet made much use of it on a professional level, but I know God had His hand in that too. The day will come when He will tell me to re-activate my passion for life coaching. God already has a plan for that, only, I cannot see when it will happen.

It was also very interesting how God had led me to my church, which you can look up in chapter 'How did I find God'. It turned my life around. I met many people who enriched my life and helped me in so many ways. When God felt I was ready, He beckoned me to get involved and contribute to our church community. During the past four years a few leadership roles came my way. Amazingly, again God was leading me and made a straight path for me to step up.

I am so grateful for all the opportunities my church is giving me to be of service and learn along the way. One never knows where these experiences will lead to one day. For now, I am busy writing this book, the book that God told me to write. I totally rely on God who will make it all possible. He promises us that when we turn to Him, He will sustain us and provide us with everything we need. Isaiah has put it in such beautiful words:

1 "Come, all you who are thirsty,
come to the waters;
and you who have no money,
come, buy and eat!
Come, buy wine and milk
without money and without cost.
2 Why spend money on what is not bread,
and your labor on what does not satisfy?
Listen, listen to me, and eat what is good,
and you will delight in the richest of fare.
Isaiah 55:1-2 (NIV)

It then continues with the assurance and promise of a happy
and fruitful life:

9 "As the heavens are higher than the Earth,
so are my ways higher than your ways
and my thoughts than your thoughts.
10 As the rain and the snow
come down from heaven,
and do not return to it
without watering the Earth
and making it bud and flourish,
so that it yields seed for the sower and bread for the eater,
11 so is my word that goes out from my mouth:
It will not return to me empty,
but will accomplish what I desire
and achieve the purpose for which I sent it.
12 You will go out in joy
and be led forth in peace;
the mountains and hills
will burst into song before you,
and all the trees of the field
will clap their hands.
Isaiah 55:9-12 (NIV)

Which points right back to the core of the
apple…God, who is all knowing

The Broom

When faced with life's trials, the natural reaction is to look for answers and work out solutions within our own strength and capabilities. Instead of carrying the burden of life by ourselves, we can turn to God for help. Our own resources are limited, but God's resources have no boundaries; there are no limits to His strength and wisdom. Imagine what can happen if you were to access His infinite strength and wisdom? All it takes is trust and belief.

I remember so clearly when, during a Sunday sermon, the pastor was saying that we needed to give up control of our life and hand it over to God. I felt every fibre in my body rejecting this idea. The concept of not being in control made me feel very uncomfortable. Though I had heard it many times before I hadn't put as much emphasis to this important message as I did that Sunday. Up until then I was quite contented to believe in God and follow Jesus. I never took into account that when one follows a person, one also submits to that person's judgement and leadership. So far I had not been ready to hand over the baton to Jesus, too scared of what He may want me to do. It can be quite unsettling when one steps out from one's own comfort zone into new and uncharted territory. What if God were to ask me to do something that I couldn't possibly do or give up something that I couldn't let go off? I just couldn't get my mind around that. I went home, with this message lingering in my heart. For many months I kept contemplating on letting go and just trusting. I kept stewing over it, knowing very well that it needed to be done sometime soon. It took a long while, but as time went on my fears slowly started to chip away.

During another sermon, our senior pastor gave us a visual demonstration with a throne and asked us this question: Who sits on the throne of your life? Are we willing to make room for Jesus and allow Him to hold the sceptre? Something shifted inside of me. It didn't sound so threatening anymore.

Perhaps it was the visual that accompanied the message. I was comforted by the assurance that Jesus will always lead me the right way. Who could possibly know better than Him? Who else is there whom I could trust with my life other than with the One that gave it to me? Since then I've been sitting next to the throne and life is much easier to deal with. The worries and difficulties of life don't appear so cumbersome anymore. Jesus said:

28 "Come to me, all you who are weary and burdened, and I will give you rest.
29 Take my yoke upon you and learn from me, for I am gentle and humble in heart, and you will find rest for your souls.
30 For my yoke is easy and my burden is light."
Matthew 11:28-30 (NIV)

Allow Jesus to carry the burdens of your life. Whenever issues or conflicts arise, I hand it over to God, completely that is. I know that after I have asked for help, I also need to let it go and leave it with God without further interference on my part.

You may have wondered what connection a Broom could have with God. It is an analogy that came to mind when I was looking for a way to illustrate why we need to let go. I actually visualised myself with a broom in my hands. Maybe you can put yourself in the picture as well:

"Imagine you have been sweeping your yard for quite a while. You carry on but the task just doesn't seem to come to an end. You now have reached the point of exhaustion and can't keep going for much longer. You are being overwhelmed by all this work.

A good friend of yours happens to walk by and notices your despair. He stops and kindly offers his help to finish up for you. You are so relieved and gladly accept his help. Your friend stretches out his hands to take over, but for some reason you are not letting go of your broom. Are you worried that your friend may not quite do it your way? Are you afraid to hand over the controls?

How can your friend possibly assist you as long as you are holding on to your precious broom? He will either ask you again or may just shrug his shoulders and continue with his walk. If you really want him to help you, the first thing that you must do is hand over your broom and step aside to give your friend the space to help you."

So it is with God. You asked and He has offered to help you. Now He waits for you to hand over the 'broom'. He cannot help you whilst you continue to hold on to your problem and still try to fix it. Only one person can handle the broom at one time. The area must be cleared to be able to be swept. Next time when you are faced with a conflict or an issue, you may want to try to remember the 'broom scenario'. Ask for help, accept, trust, let go and step aside to make room for God to take over. Sit back and let God help and guide you.

What I have experienced so far is that by giving up control, God will never ask me to do the impossible. God would never ask us to do anything that we are not able to do. He has given us all unique talents and gifts and knows exactly what we are capable of. He is aware of all our weaknesses and strengths.

Would parents ask the impossible of their children or worse, put them in situations that might be harmful to them? They only want the best for their children, so does God.

Giving up control allows you the space and time to 'soften' up. You no longer have to carry the whole burden by yourself. So often when I asked for help, the solution came so quickly that it took me by surprise. Why haven't I thought about this myself? But there are times when God appears not to be doing anything. Then you may wonder whether He has heard your prayer at all. Is He ever going to do anything or has He even forgotten? Impatience can drive most people into taking matters back into their own hands. But you can rest assured, God has perfect timing and there will always be a solution. Sometimes it may be later than sooner...

A few months back, I had some serious issues at work. I came home one evening after work, feeling totally out of sorts. I was in a space that I desperately wanted to escape from. It kept having a grip on me and tried to drag me down even further. All I felt was that I wanted to immerse myself in 'God space'. I took my dog and went out for a walk. I put on my headphones and tuned into my favourite Christian radio station. It took a long hard walk, a couple of inspiring teaching programmes and some worship songs for me to settle down. My spirit started to lift and I felt my inner peace return.

On my way back I felt ready to pray and I asked God for help. I remembered my 'Broom' story and consciously let go of the problem. I asked God to make sure that I would clearly understand what, if or when I needed to do anything. So I patiently waited. Often thoughts of unease would creep in, but I would dismiss them, careful to not interfere. I replaced the negativities with things I love.

Nothing much seemed to happen during the following days. I imagined all sorts of different scenarios of how this conflict was going to be straightened out. But as the weeks passed by, the whole issue resolved itself in a very uncanny way. The person I was in conflict with was transferred and it never even came to the dreaded confrontation. I was so relieved that all panned out so perfectly without any effort on my part. All I had to do was step aside, wait and let God do the sweeping. Imagine what would have happened had I handled this situation myself. It certainly would not have had the same outcome.

Something I read:

> If God answers your prayer,
> He increases your faith
>
> If God lets you wait,
> He increases your patience
>
> If God doesn't answer your prayer
> He has something better for you

Whatever the outcome, it will be for your best interest. God wants you to achieve and flourish. He will make sure that His plans for you will come to fruition. It is in His best interest that you succeed because it fits into His Grand Plan. Do not have any expectations on time or outcome, trust and let God act on your behalf.

> *Trust in the LORD with all your heart*
> *and lean not on your own understanding;*
> *in all your ways submit to him,*
> *and he will make your paths straight.*
> *Proverb 3:5-6 (NIV)*

My prayer:

Dear Father in Heaven, thank you that you love me.
Thank you that I can pass on all my worries and
burdens over to you.
I know that you will take care of me with the best
possible outcome for all involved.
Thank you Jesus for the freedom that you have given
me to accomplish what I'm called to do. I no longer
need to worry and be filled with unnecessary fear.
Thank you for giving me strength, courage and
confidence to tackle all that lies ahead.
Thank you Lord that I am so privileged in my life
and I pray that you continue to provide me with
everything I need.
God, I trust You and I place my life completely into
Your hands."

Amen

Which points right back to the core of the
apple…God, who strengthens us and gives us
counsel in all situations

What do I pack for my Journey Home?

People say that life is not fair. I think life **is** fair. By that I'm not saying that life is easy. Nor am I implying that sickness, addictions, loss, grieve, pain, wars, crime, or violence are not a part of life. The simple truth is that there has never been anyone who was capable of 'cheating' life. We are all in the same boat and have to die someday. When we do, we cannot take ANYTHING with us, no matter who we are, who we know and what we have. Nor does anyone have the advantage of earning or paying for God's favour. There are no tickets to eternal life for sale. Everyone is equal, regardless of status, heritage, wealth or power.

The purpose of life is to prepare us for our next stop on our journey to eternity. Not unlike going away on a vacation or business trip, we need to prepare ourselves and plan a destination, buy tickets, organise a passport, work out our travel routes and the necessary transport and accommodation. Last but not least, we pack our bags with everything we will require on our voyage.

When my mother died, I flew back to Switzerland to say farewell. Arriving at her apartment with my brother, for some odd reason I felt strange. As I walked into the living room, my mother's personal things were still on the table but she wasn't there. Somehow I expected that all would have disappeared together with my mum. A peculiar thought entered my mind: "Why couldn't you take all this with you mum?"

Later on my brother took me to the morgue. When I looked at my mother I expected her face to be engraved with pain from all the years of suffering with her MS and the hardship she had to endure in her life, raising four children on her own. To my surprise my mother's face looked peaceful and contented. It was as if she wanted to tell me that she had achieved and done everything in her life that she came here to do.

I felt so relieved that she was able to pass on with a "fait accompli". I believe that in the end she realised that she had done very well. She had brought up four healthy children who are all doing well, leading an upright life, neither involved in drugs or crime.

What is it that we can actually take with us? What legacy will we leave behind? In my mother's case, she has taken with her the assurance that she has given us a sound foundation to do well in life and to live by the right morals and standards she had instilled in us. She left good memories but also some sad and upsetting ones. Her grandchildren and we are her legacy. I felt odd and very sad to sift through my mother's possessions that didn't really belong to me.

This awareness underlines how important it is to consider what truly matters in life and how feeble worldly achievements and acquisitions really are. We all know very well that once we go, we cannot take anything with us. Each time someone close dies, we get reminded: All that is missing is the person; everything else remains behind.

So, what exactly is it that we *can* pack? We need to shift our attention from what is important to us to what it is important to God. As we do this we are changing from a single-minded attitude to a collective awareness.

2 After fasting forty days and forty nights, he was hungry.
3 The tempter came to him and said, "If you are the Son of God, tell these stones to become bread."
4 Jesus answered, "It is written: 'Man shall not live on bread alone, but on every word that comes from the mouth of God.' "
Matthew 4:2-4 (NIV)

Jesus had just spent 40 days without food and water in the desert. He would have been starving and at His tether. The devil (tempter) took this moment as his golden opportunity to tempt Jesus. Of course Jesus could have turned anything to bread but He stood His ground. He put His own physical desire (hunger) second to what was important to God, His Father in Heaven. He is teaching us that physical needs are only short lived but our souls are forever. God is not just providing us with physical sustenance; He also nurtures our soul so that we can draw closer to Him and to know Him. He wants us to learn what to pack to take with us. It certainly is not money and power. It's all about contributing, reaching out to our fellow men and to do whatever we are born to do. This is where we can set our God-given talents into action:

be compassionate
care for the elderly
be a healer for the sick
forgive & pray for others
feed the hungry - look after the poor - pray for the fallen
bring hope to the hopeless - be a companion for the lonely
share the good news to the unbeliever - be the light in the dark
listen to the forgotten
don't forget the widow
give water to the thirsty
take care of the orphan
bring joy to the mourner
be forthcoming to others
show the way for the lost
give shelter to the homeless
be a servant of God's Kingdom

*Each time you make someone's face light up with a grateful smile,
you know that you have placed something else into your bag.*

*Each time you change someone's life,
you know that you live with a true purpose.*

*Each time you can stop someone from crying,
you know that God is in your heart.*

Monica

The Nature Strip

"On my way to the park, I used to pass a house that belonged to a man called Angelo. Often I would stop to have a chat with him. Angelo was a very kind and friendly man who enjoyed company as well as helping others. He used to cut the grass for a lady across the road. Sometimes he would walk up the road and we often crossed paths.

Two or three years had passed and Angelo became fragile. He told me that he was getting dizzy and not feeling too well. I saw less and less of him whereas before he would always work on something in his beautiful garden or around the house. It would always look immaculate. I missed seeing him. Then one day, his son had to take him away to a nursing home. Angelo was no longer able to live by himself. Gradually the empty house and garden started to appear disorderly and kind of looked lost.

Weeks later when I walked past, I was saddened by what I saw. There was a huge 'pile' of Angelo's stuff thrown on the nature strip to be picked up and taken to the tip by the council. Here in Australia we tend to sift through those kinds of piles to see if there is anything we can still use. I was rather upset to see some of his furniture, knickknacks, dishes and bits and pieces tossed out on the road.

All through his life he acquired his little treasures and memorabilia and kept them in his home. These were things that he would have held dear. Now that he was gone, it had become worthless to others. These worldly things that he would have worked so hard for are now meaningless to others. Most people would have walked past this 'heap of rubble' and wouldn't have given it a second thought, assuming that the occupants may have had a bit of a spring clean. But I saw a man's life being 'disposed' of, because I was aware of who used to live in this house."

This heart-rending event made me think of this chapter. It reminded me of just how worthless our worldly possessions really are. Is this all we can leave behind, a pile of dross that no one cares for, tossed out on a nature strip? Or perhaps is it a pile of money, precious jewellery or properties that people will fight over? But if you collect and pack the right 'stuff' during your stay on this planet, you can be certain that it won't be found on any nature strip. It will be treasured in eternity, awaiting awards beyond your imagination. I truly believe God's Kingdom is worth fighting for. Here are the words of Jesus:

19 "Do not store up for yourselves treasures on Earth, where moths and vermin destroy, and where thieves break in and steal.
20 But store up for yourselves treasures in heaven, where moths and vermin do not destroy, and where thieves do not break in and steal.
21 For where your treasure is, there your heart will be also.
Matthew 6:19-21 (NIV)

This whole episode made me very sad and it opened my eyes. Is it not much wiser to let go of something now rather than having it go to waste? Do we really need to hang on to everything we possess?

It weighs much more than gold to give someone a heartfelt smile. How does it make you feel to see how little it takes to make someone happy with *only* one a smile? Often it doesn't require much to help a person through a difficult situation. To exchange a word or two with an elderly or lonely person and offer a hand to someone in need, that is what gives us access to the key that unlocks God's boundless treasure chest.

Every day gives us plenty of opportunities to reach out in some ways. This is the sort of 'dross' we want leave behind, but it will be embedded in people's hearts forever instead of being discarded on the side of the road.

One way to get started is by spending time reading the Bible and praying daily. It 'feeds your soul' with God's words and strengthens you in your pursuit of changing your life, making what is important to God important to you. All it takes is <u>one</u> decision to move forward and grow with Jesus. Make it a daily habit to spend time with God by reading for just 10-15 minutes every day. The best way to form a new '*habit*' is to attach it to an existing routine/habit. For instance, each morning you get up and most likely have a coffee or a cup of tea with your breakfast. Maybe you read the newspaper or watch the Good Morning Show on TV. All you need to do is have your coffee as usual and pin on your new 'God habit'. Perhaps you can read some passages in the train going to work? During your lunch break you could sit somewhere quiet and spend some time reading a couple of verses. You can find plenty of opportunities to set aside a few precious minutes in your day.

Praying is even easier. It can be done everywhere and anytime. Walking the dog, tending to your garden, standing in a queue, in the car, riding the bicycle, at the beach, in the bathroom, at the gym, cooking dinner... God can hear you anywhere. If you want God to play the main role in your life, you would want to get to know Him and learn from Him. Slowly you will notice the changes that are happening within and around you.

At some point we do need to get our bags ready. When will you decide to start packing? What have you stashed away in your suitcase so far? Remember, unlike your summer vacation, you have no ETA on your final departure.

Which points right back to the core of the apple...God, our final destination

The Museum

What does it matter how much money we have and what possessions we have accumulated? What difference does it make whether we have a Rolls Royce or a big diamond ring on our finger when we die?

What we perceive as gain only applies in the worldly existence,
In the afterlife it is worthless, without meaning.
Consider well what you will lose in the pursuit of worldly gains.
Monica

Here on Earth, we can side step and cheat our way through life. We can lie and steal to get what we want, convinced that we have succeeded. But we cannot cheat death. Some people may think they can weasel their way through life by gaining power and money and to rule over others. But when death knocks on the door, the picture changes and one's own will and control comes to a stop.

Hopes placed in mortals die with them; all the promise of their power comes to nothing.
Proverbs 11:7 (NIV)

Life is like a museum. It is wondrous and fascinating. We can enjoy and learn from all the precious and valuable artifacts on display. Some items we can even get to touch. We can stay all day but inevitably comes the time for the final call. We all must leave and then all the doors get shut. On our way out, we cannot take anything with us. We leave exactly as we came in. Everything remains at the museum, ready for other people who will visit the next day, weeks, months and years to follow.

The time we spend at the museum is our lifetime. When the lights go out, we must leave. The artifacts and all the treasures we admired are the remnants and legacies of our ancestors. One day, the next generation will visit and 'admire' our footprints and contributions we left behind. What is it that we want them to see? The level of enjoyment and appreciation on their walk through the museum all depends on what it is we are doing with ourselves, to and for others and how we treat our environment.

It is not up to the janitor to choose what is being exhibited. He only cares for the exhibits and keeps them well maintained. The museum solely relies on donations and new discoveries that are constantly being added to the collection. The real possessions we need to accumulate are the things that really matter. A life of exuberant luxury and overabundance is not a very suitable playing field. It is so easy to be blinded by all the glitter and glamour of the world. It only causes us to set the wrong priorities, influenced by superficial pleasures and treasures, which only lead to self-deception.

7 Do not be deceived: God cannot be mocked. A man reaps what he sows.
8 Whoever sows to please their flesh, from the flesh will reap destruction; whoever sows to please the Spirit, from the Spirit will reap eternal life.
Galatians 6:7-8 (NIV)

In the Gospel of Mark we find the story of a very rich man who asked Jesus: "What must I do to inherit eternal life?" In other words, how he can gain entry to the Kingdom of God ("what does he have to pack"). All through his life he had kept all the commandments and led an upright life:

20 "Teacher," he declared, "all these I have kept since I was a boy."
21 Jesus looked at him and loved him. "One thing you lack," he said. "Go, sell everything you have and give to the poor,

and you will have treasure in heaven. Then come, follow me."
22 At this the man's face fell. He went away sad, because he had great wealth.
23 Jesus looked around and said to his disciples, "How hard it is for the rich to enter the kingdom of God!"
Mark 13:20-23 (NIV)

There is nothing that this world can offer that unlocks the door to God's Kingdom. Whatever we possess, we have received through the Grace of God. He is the One who equipped us with the abilities to achieve what we gained. But it is up to us how and where we choose to put our strength into practice. Is it just for self or do we consider others? Jesus has explained this in a very colourful parable with the story of the ten virgins:

1 "At that time the kingdom of heaven will be like ten virgins who took their lamps and went out to meet the bridegroom.
2 Five of them were foolish and five were wise.
3 The foolish ones took their lamps but did not take any oil with them.
4 The wise ones, however, took oil in jars along with their lamps.
5 The bridegroom was a long time in coming, and they all became drowsy and fell asleep.
6 "At midnight the cry rang out: 'Here's the bridegroom! Come out to meet him!'
7 "Then all the virgins woke up and trimmed their lamps.
8 The foolish ones said to the wise, 'Give us some of your oil; our lamps are going out.'
9 " 'No,' they replied, 'there may not be enough for both us and you. Instead, go to those who sell oil and buy some for yourselves.'
10 "But while they were on their way to buy the oil, the bridegroom arrived. The virgins who were ready went in with him to the wedding banquet. And the door was shut.
11 "Later the others also came. 'Lord, Lord,' they said, 'open the door for us!' "But he replied,
12 'Truly I tell you, I don't know you.'

*13 "Therefore keep watch, because you do not know the day
or the hour.
Matthew 25:1-13 (NIV)*

Have you replenished your oilcan? The following verses of Psalm show just how fleeting our life is in contrast to the collective existence of all the ages past and yet to come. Make the most of it and chase after what <u>really</u> matters.

*4 "Show me, LORD, my life's end and the number of my days;
let me know how fleeting my life is.
5 You have made my days a mere handbreadth;
the span of my years is as nothing before you.
Everyone is but a breath, even those who seem secure.
6 "Surely everyone goes around like a mere phantom;
in vain they rush about,
heaping up wealth without knowing whose it will finally be.
7 "But now, LORD, what do I look for?
My hope is in you.
Psalm 39:4-7 (NIV)*

Ecclesiastes is a rather pragmatic book. It highlights all the elements that divert our attention from the essential and true purpose of life. King Solomon wrote Ecclesiastes. He was the richest man and the most revered king that ever walked on this Earth. God had gifted him with wisdom that far surpassed people of his time. He says that there was nothing he hadn't done in his life. He had tried everything possible under the sun.

In the end we need to face the fact that it all means nothing as we have to leave it all behind. What counts is how we stand with God. Let's have a look what King Solomon says. He warns us not to waste our life:

Toil is meaningless

1 So I hated life, because the work that is done under the sun was grievous to me. All of it is meaningless, a chasing after the wind.

18 I hated all the things I had toiled for under the sun, because I must leave them to the one who comes after me.
19 And who knows whether that person will be wise or foolish? Yet they will have control over all the fruit of my toil into which I have poured my effort and skill under the sun. This too is meaningless.
20 So my heart began to despair over all my toilsome labor under the sun. 21. For a person may labor with wisdom, knowledge and skill, and then they must leave all they own to another who has not toiled for it. This too is meaningless and a great misfortune.
22 What do people get for all the toil and anxious striving with which they labor under the sun?
23 All their days their work is grief and pain; even at night their minds do not rest. This too is meaningless.
24 A person can do nothing better than to eat and drink and find satisfaction in their own toil. This too, I see, is from the hand of God,
25 for without him, who can eat or find enjoyment?
26 To the person who pleases him, God gives wisdom, knowledge and happiness, but to the sinner he gives the task of gathering and storing up wealth to hand it over to the one who pleases God. This too is meaningless, a chasing after the wind.
Ecclesiastes 2:17-26 (NIV)

There is so much wisdom and insight in these verses. He would have been of quite an advanced age. I love the expression "a chasing after the wind". Have you ever tried to chase the wind?

It expresses it so well: What exactly are we trying to achieve (=chasing) in life? As long as we go after the 'worldly' (=wind) stuff, we will never catch it, because it is meaningless and will not last. You can only "borrow" it for a short time, for when you die it will no longer be yours. The world is like the wind, for one moment it blows in your face to give you pleasure and then drifts away and disappears. What is it that you are chasing after? Is it the wind? Has anyone ever been able to catch the wind? Why then is it that we continue trying so hard? How lucky are we to have such teachings readily available. Do we take heed or do we just continue on in life as we have so far?

The essence of this book really lies in the chapters "*Why God*" and "*Why Jesus*" but after the "Why" we also need the "How". This is what makes this chapter so important. It gives us the "how" and "what is next".

That is why it was so difficult to choose only a few of the many Bible verses relating to this chapter. It is for a good reason that God is alluding to this throughout the Old and New Testament in so many ways. It is evident throughout the history of the Israelites, the prophecies and advice from the prophets, the parables spoken by Jesus and the teachings that followed from the apostles. The whole Bible is an example of:

- How God kept all His promises to people who followed him
- The examples of what happened to people who have ignored God
- A template of how we need to look at life
- Signposts of how to lead an upright and worthwhile life
- Warnings
- Prophesies fulfilled and yet to be fulfilled

Yes, it is to be taken seriously how we prepare ourselves and what we pack for our journey home. It will determine our final destination. It is like eating the apple; you always end up at its core. Life is just like it. When our physical body expires, we return to where we came from, back to the core, back to the Creator.

Whilst we spend time on Earth, it is up to us to choose what it is that we want to pursue. Is it to fulfill our own selfish desires such as wealth, fame and power or is it to quench our inner thirst to fill our 'God Space' in our hearts? Do we want to align ourselves with the spiritual reality?

What can you take with you when you depart? How important is it what you leave behind in the hands of your heirs and to strangers? The end-effect is what you want to satisfy, your body or your spirit? As one grows older, the need of acquiring possessions diminishes and other values are pushed to the foreground. I guess we can all feel that the days left are getting fewer and we'd better start packing before it is too late altogether.

The world conditions us to believe that the more money and power one has, the more important and respected one becomes. Our self worth is measured by what we have accomplished and by what we possess. Look at all the movies, games and daily media bombardment we are subjected to. It starts as soon as children open their eyes. Is there any wonder that we totally lose reality? In a sense it could be a bit like the movie called "*Matrix*". I'm sure some of you remember it. Quite scary to think that our world as we know it could just be an illusion. In some ways it is, only that the reality is of course not like the one portrayed in *Matrix*. Our reality is to find our own core, our Creator.

This analogy perfectly illustrates that we are all equal. What difference does it make how much one has acquired or what social status one is in? The story will always end the same:

You see 2 coffins in front of you. In one coffin lies a multibillionaire. He is in his most expensive suit and all done up to look his best.

In the other coffin rests a person who had no worldly possessions, in fact he was a homeless beggar. He lies there in his best suit, which has seen better days, all frayed and faded. His face is drawn and pale.

What can you see? Which of the two men is better off? Is there even a difference? Which one of these men has control over the journey ahead?

Is the coffin with the gold handles and mahogany wood going to assist the rich man to reach the Kingdom of God? What happens to the unstained and rough looking coffin with the rope handles? Is this coffin unable to take the beggar to the Kingdom of God?

This confronting example shows that neither man receives any special treatment and privileges. God is not interested in the outward appearance. He purely focuses on the treasures in the hearts of people.

He will only welcome a pure spirit / soul. What sort of spirit are you cultivating?

Rich and poor have this in common:
The LORD is the Maker of them all.

Proverbs 22:2 (NIV)

Which points right back to the core of the apple...God, who only looks at your heart

Space Odyssey

A Human cannot see beyond his earthly life, himself being the centrepiece.

Here I would like to engage you in a fun exercise. This little adventure will open up a different view to your own perspective: It takes you from your own significance and existence to being a part of an infinite co-existence, past, present and future.

Go through each step and with your eyes closed, imagine the pictures as vividly as you can. Don't move to the next step until the images have fully emerged in your mind:

1. Imagine yourself being born, being a little baby. **The picture you see is that of you and your parents.** YOU are the centrepiece, filling up most of your picture.

2. As you grow older, you start to take notice of your family and neighbours. **The picture you see is expanding and you see yourself within a small community.** It becomes part of your environment; you slowly zoom out. Your own person starts to decrease in size.

3. Then imagine yourself as an adult and increase your periphery to the city and state you live in. **The picture you see now is that of a bird's view of yourself in the middle of a crowd of people mingling in your city.** Your own person becomes smaller still.

4. Now begin to see yourself within your country amongst everyone else. **The picture you see now has turned into a map of your country, with you in it somewhere.** You may just be able to make out where your home is located.

5.   Now you visualise yourself in a spacecraft, lifting off the ground and hovering over your country and then around the rest of the globe. **The picture you see now is that of our Planet Earth.** Can you still make out where you are?

6.   It doesn't stop there. Lift up even higher and further away from Earth. You are looking at our solar system. **The picture you see now is that of Earth almost disappearing amongst other and bigger planets.** Where are you now?

7.   If you still want to go further, travel even deeper into space. **The picture you see now is that you can't make out our solar system anymore.** The sun and our planet Earth are no longer visible from where you are.

By each of these steps, you remove yourself from YOU. It takes you on a journey from being the centre of YOUR universe to being a part of THE universe. You begin to realise that your whole being and life is even smaller than a drop in the ocean and that other lives are all the other drops that fill the same ocean.

As humans, we tend to pay too much attention to ourselves and our own needs and desires. This exercise can help you to shift your focus towards others and your environment.

What would happen if you were to apply the same technique to your everyday life? It can work for you in exactly the same way. The further you distance yourself from your own problems, the smaller and less significant they become. This levels the playing field and allows you to take notice of other people's dilemmas:

"The picture you see now is that of a lot of other people who also do it tough in life."

Whose problems are more important? None are more

significant than others, they are all important in God's view. The point is that they all have various degrees of implications. You can start to ask yourself how your own problems fit in with the rest. Could it be that others may be much worse off?

By removing the focus from your own problems and directing it onto others is just like noticing other and bigger planets. Your own 'planet' starts to fit into a collective picture. How? By looking at yourself from a greater distance with less focus, your problems won't cloud your mind so much. It empowers you to deal with difficult situations much better. The mind (brain) is created to survive and find solutions, but from time to time it needs a 'disc cleanup' and a 'defrag', just like a computer. When unnecessary files clutter up the system, it starts to freeze up.

Keep your mind fresh by acknowledging your issues but not to stay focused on them. Instead, widen your periphery to include others. You can't but feel compelled to reach out and help. In turn, others will reach out and help YOU. This is the outcome of one of the commandments; *love your neighbour as yourself*. What comes around goes around.

"The picture you see now is that of other people in dire need of food, clothes and shelter and whose lives are endangered."

What does it matter if you have the latest TV set or the newest car? What about that insistent flu that you had for the past week or two? Or your boss that has not been treating you fairly? Maybe you can't afford to go on a much-earned holiday? At the end of your days, what does it all matter?

Does it not matter more how you fit into the whole picture or what you set your focus on in life? We are all part of God's universe. Our Creator has placed your soul into a physical body and is waiting for you to realise that you can simply connect to Him by focusing on what it is that you have been created for.

Look at the Ten Commandments again. You will realise that they all lead to the same conclusion, treat others as you want to be treated. One day when this happens there will be harmony, love and understanding between all nations on Earth.

Ever tried to build a house of cards? It needs _ALL_ the cards to be in perfect balance and harmony. Pull just one out of place and watch it tumble down. Dismiss or ignore only one of the commandments and it too will come tumbling down. Only, you won't realise it until it is too late.

How carefully do you place your cards? **What picture do you see now when you are looking at your life (house of cards)?**

Which points right back to the core of the apple…God, who commands all the planets but still never loses sight of you

God given Gifts and Talents

So what happens when people start to understand more and more why they need to be with, rather than against God? Yet more questions will start to surface and this can get a bit tricky:

- Where do I fit in?
- What am I supposed to do?
- What has God planned for me?
- What is my calling?
- What are my true strengths and talents?
- How can I find out what they are?

God has provided us all with gifts and talents to do what we are born to do. They make us unique. We all have a destiny that God has planned for us so that we can bear fruit and prosper. He has made sure to equip us with the right tools. We are all meant to contribute somehow and somewhere within society. Your special gifts are within you, waiting to be discovered. It is your very own toolbox.

Do you know what tools God has placed in your toolbox? Many of us have already discovered our talents, some are uncertain and others are not even aware that they have a special gift. There are people who may never have had the opportunity or courage to apply their talents yet.

There are many ways to find out. A good start is to ask God to help you in the process. Often one can literally 'stumble over' a special gift by accident. This is exactly what happened to me during one of my visits to Switzerland 12 years ago.

My sister treated both of us to a specialised spinal massage (Breuss massage). I asked my sister to be treated first. I just sat there observing. Before long I started to get very interested. I began to ask a lot of questions. The therapist was very obliging and was happy to answer my questions. On our way back to my sister's house all I could think was that I too wanted to massage people from my home.

As soon as I arrived back in Melbourne, I went ahead with my plans without delay. I ordered a massage table made to measure, organised the oils, towels and set up my room. I told my friends and for first few weeks started off with the Breuss massage. It didn't take long and the table was paid for. As soon as the new school year began, I looked for a massage school in the Yellow Pages. I found a terrific teacher who was very talented and inspiring. Along the way I was also able to learn from my fellow students.

This was my initial plan, but as time went on, I discovered that this was in fact one of my talents. I was no longer satisfied with 'just' massaging. I wanted to learn more to be able to fix the actual cause of the pain rather than treating the effect. A massage in itself often cannot accomplish this. 'The more you know, the more you know what you don't know'.

The saying goes: "When the student is ready, the teacher will appear." And so it happened. Everything I touched worked out so effortlessly. Just like a jigsaw puzzle, it all started to fall into place. I had no difficulties learning. The human anatomy and its functionality were like second nature to me. Even without studying anatomy I was able to sense what was wrong and how to adjust it. It took me a bit by surprise and it still does.

God has given me this wonderful gift, which has enabled me to help numerous people with problems where other therapists and doctors were unsuccessful. To this day I'm privileged to witness miracles and wonders that fill my heart with a humble gratitude towards God who has honoured me with such a wonderful and worthy gift.

It was quite obvious that it was God's plan. He has equipped me with everything I needed to be able to help my clients. I never had to struggle for anything. Nothing stood in the way for me to advance my skills further. He revealed to me a talent that I was unaware of. Funnily enough, years later a few of my relatives did mention to me that they had noticed this gift of helping people and the compassion to reach out to others in me as a child.

When you attempt to acquire a new skill and you find it easy to learn; that would most likely indicate your calling in life. If the opposite occurs it is best to let go and keep searching. There is no need to exert yourself and persist in trying to excel in something that is not one of your strengths and completely goes against the grain. Don't waste your time and energy with things you are struggling with. Pray and trust God, He will point you in the right direction, and then just follow the prompts. Prompts may come through new people you meet, an article you may read or a strong feeling that compels you to explore a new area that you would never have thought of before. It may be something that you feel you could never do. It may even be a complete contrast to your usual occupation.

This book is yet another good example because I have never written a book. The closest that came to any writing experience would have been the research project I had to compile as part of the life-coaching certificate. But when I was convinced that God wanted me to go ahead, I put my trust fully in Him and got underway. I never worried about the steps ahead. I knew God would give me the right ideas of how to proceed. And this is exactly what happened. Whenever I reached a particular stage of completion, the next steps would continue to unfold. Not at any point was I left without guidance.

Our God given talents are to be cherished and utilised in gratitude. You can only truly flourish if they are being applied in the name of the giver, our God. The results will be fruitful and beneficial to oneself as well as others.

We need to determine if they have a purpose that will have a positive impact on others and society. What are the intentions and desired outcomes based on? How would one interact as successful person? Is it in line with God?

So what kind of talents are we looking for? Are there any 'wrong' ones? I believe that if it is for the greater good, how could anything possibly be wrong. Exceptional people who can perform these tasks with great skills occupy every imaginable field of expertise and service. It is yet another way that God shows us the perfection of His Creation. He does not miss anything and all is distributed accordingly. This is why the Bible tells us not to compare ourselves with others, we are all distinct individuals set out to do our part. Love and unleash your own talents; thrive and be the best YOU can be:

- Art
- Music
- Science
- Business
- Health Care
- Aged, Child & Disability Care
- Research & Development
- Building & Construction
- Education
- Clergies and priests
- Hospitality
- Government
- Public Services
- Transport
- Banking & Finance
- Farming & Agriculture
- Trade Labourers
- Sports & Leisure
- Missionaries
- Undertakers

These are only a few, but there are many more areas where one can avail one's own strengths and unique skills. Talents and gifts always come in conjunction with passion and love. How could anyone excel in anything in the absence of zeal and enthusiasm?

Everything we think and do will affect others. Every decision we make impacts other lives and every single human being matters. We may sometimes tend to think that we are not important, but every action causes a ripple effect.

I love to watch the movie called "It's a wonderful Life" during the Christmas season. It was released in December 1946 and tells about a man that is disgruntled and disappointed with his life. The movie shows 2 parallel lives, one is with the man in it and the other scenario plays out without His existence. The lives of people in this town turned out totally different. It is well worth watching as it portrays how a person's talents and gifts influence the lives of everyone in a positive way, even if we cannot see it ourselves. It also indicates that even if we don't always give ourselves enough credit, others do.

In the New Testament, Jesus uses a parable of the three servants. It teaches us what will happen when our talents go to waste. These servants received different amounts of Gold from their master. The NIV (New International Version) translates it as *bags* of Gold, but the ESV (English Standard Version) calls it *talents*. It both relates to a measure but it is a rather interesting play on words that fits perfectly.

14 "For it will be like a man going on a journey, who called his servants and entrusted to them his property.
15 To one he gave five talents, to another two, to another one, to each according to his ability. Then he went away.
16 He who had received the five talents went at once and traded with them, and he made five talents more.
17 So also he who had the two talents made two talents more.
18 But he who had received the one talent went and dug in

the ground and hid his master's money.
19 Now after a long time the master of those servants came and settled accounts with them.
20 And he who had received the five talents came forward, bringing five talents more, saying, 'Master, you delivered to me five talents; here I have made five talents more.'
21 His master said to him, 'Well done, good and faithful servant. You have been faithful over a little; I will set you over much. Enter into the joy of your master.'
22 And he also who had the two talents came forward, saying, 'Master, you delivered to me two talents; here I have made two talents more.'
23 His master said to him, 'Well done, good and faithful servant. You have been faithful over a little; I will set you over much. Enter into the joy of your master.'
24 He also who had received the one talent came forward, saying, 'Master, I knew you to be a hard man, reaping where you did not sow, and gathering where you scattered no seed,
25 so I was afraid, and I went and hid your talent in the ground. Here you have what is yours.'
26 But his master answered him, 'You wicked and slothful servant! You knew that I reap where I have not sown and gather where I scattered no seed?
27 Then you ought to have invested my money with the bankers, and at my coming I should have received what was my own with interest.
28 So take the talent from him and give it to him who has the ten talents.
29 For to everyone who has will more be given, and he will have an abundance. But from the one who has not, even what he has will be taken away.
Matthew 25:14-29 (ESV)

This example shows how God selects and blesses His people with unique abilities in the Old Testament:

1 Then the LORD said to Moses,
2 "See, I have chosen Bezalel son of Uri, the son of Hur, of

the tribe of Judah,
3 and I have filled him with the Spirit of God, with wisdom,
with understanding, with knowledge and with all kinds of
skills—
4 to make artistic designs for work in gold, silver and bronze,
5 to cut and set stones, to work in wood, and to engage in all
kinds of crafts.
6 Moreover, I have appointed Oholiab son of Ahisamak, of
the tribe of Dan, to help him. Also I have given ability to all
the skilled workers to make everything I have commanded
you:
Exodus 31:1-6 (NIV)

From there it goes on in detail concerning what needed to be done.

God chooses each of us to play a certain role as part of the collective existence. We all are a piece of an enormous puzzle that will, in the end, be perfectly completed. We may not understand nor see how and when it can happen, but trust God, He can. After His resurrection, Jesus appeared to His chosen apostles numerous times. He tells that they will all be given gifts through His Holy Spirit:

4 On one occasion, while he was eating with them, he gave
them this command: "Do not leave Jerusalem, but wait for
the gift my Father promised, which you have heard me speak
about.
5 For John baptized with water, but in a few days you will be
baptized with the Holy Spirit."
Act 1:4-5 (NIV)

They all trusted, prayed and waited for it to happen. God always keeps His promises and this is how His Holy Spirit manifested itself:

2 Suddenly a sound like the blowing of a violent wind came
from heaven and filled the whole house where they were
sitting.
3 They saw what seemed to be tongues of fire that separated

and came to rest on each of them.
4 All of them were filled with the Holy Spirit and began to
speak in other tongues as the Spirit enabled them.
Act 1:2-4 (NIV)

These verses describe the kinds of gifts we can receive:

7 Now to each one the manifestation of the Spirit is given for
the common good.
*8 To one there is given through the Spirit a **message of***
***wisdom**, to another a **message of knowledge** by means of*
the same Spirit,
*9 to another **faith** by the same Spirit, to another **gifts of***
***healing** by that one Spirit,*
*10 to another **miraculous powers**, to another **prophecy,** to*
*another **distinguishing between spirits**, to another*
***speaking in different kinds of tongues**, and to still another*
*the **interpretation of tongues**.*
11 All these are the work of one and the same Spirit, and he
distributes them to each one, just as he determines.
1 Corinthians 12:4-11 (NIV)

All these gifts equip us to thrive and excel in areas that each person is 'assigned' to. But we must always remember that they are only meant for the good of people and the Kingdom of God. Like any gifts we receive, we must honour, treasure and respect them.

Throughout the four Gospels we read how Jesus had compassion for others. He set His own needs aside and never used His power for His own benefit; His only concern was to help others. All our personal 'power' has been granted and given to us by the Grace of God. This is what Jesus said to Pilate before He was sentenced:

Jesus answered, "You would have no power over me if it
were not given to you from above.
Therefore the one who handed me over to you is guilty of a
greater sin."
John 19:11 (NIV)

God doesn't use 'perfect' people to work for his Kingdom. Really, how is perfection defined anyway? It is not up to us to decide. We are all perfect in the eyes of our Creator. He knows all His raw diamonds, even the ones that have diverged and gotten lost.

The best example is that of the apostle Paul, who used to be called Saul. God transformed him from a fervent and feared Christian prosecutor to a sincerely devoted apostle who even ended up writing most of the New Testament. It is never too late to change, regardless of age and abilities. No one is ever too far gone as not to be found by God.

Do you know what talents you have? Do you know who you are? What are the areas that you feel you can do better at than the average person? If you are not sure where your actual strengths lie, think of what type of hobbies you have. They often are a good indicator. Sometimes a busy lifestyle may not always allow for extra time to indulge in such activities.

People tend to forget their childhood dreams. It may help you to re-visit your long forgotten memories as a child and explore what your ideologies, hopes and ambitions were. Children's imaginations flow free without any self-limiting thoughts. The best ideas come from such thinking: nothing is impossible.

As adults we forget to dream. Life does have the tendency to rob us of our aspirations and hopes. We lower the bar on our expectations to adjust and cope with the disappointments.

Set yourself back to these carefree years and remember what it was like then. What was it that made your heart burn with excitement? It will still be there, buried under the daily grind of life. These dreams may just be what you are born to do.

God gives you the freedom and self-confidence to learn about yourself because he created you and He knows you. To 'find' yourself you need to find God first. Talk to God and ask Him for help. There is no better feeling than to know that one has found one's true purpose in life. From this point on it will be much easier to navigate through life in a steadfast pace. You just have to follow the dotted line and don't have to worry about any "what ifs" or "what happens after?" All will be revealed to you in the appropriate time. The big questions no longer restrict you with uncertainties and doubts. It gives your life true meaning when you are synchronised with God. You are 'tuned' in to your Creator and play your part in the **collective existence**.

You are free to follow through with any task and know that even before you have completed it, the next thing is already waiting for you. You will receive all the blessings you need from God. This is what Jesus refers to when He promises us freedom. This makes us 'servants of God's Kingdom'. Being a servant of God is fulfilling one's own purpose in God's name: To do what one is born and destined to do and to serve mankind. If it is God's will, you cannot fail.

God's dimension has no need for materialism, nothing to chase after, no self-glorification, no prestige and no power. We will exist in total harmony within the Glory of God.

Life here on Earth is to learn and acknowledge these facts and to prepare us for a wondrous journey ahead. Whoever is not prepared to learn and grow will be left behind. Being disconnected from God would not be a very promising providence to look forward to.

We have to keep in mind that ultimately God is in control. We need to carefully evaluate how and where we apply our gifts and talents.

Which points right back to the core of the apple…God, the Giver of gifts and Source of our strength, who blesses us to be a blessing for others

Ask and you shalt receive

7 "Ask and it will be given to you; seek and you will find; knock and the door will be opened to you.
8 For everyone who asks receives; the one who seeks finds; and to the one who knocks, the door will be opened.

Matthew 7:7-8 (NIV)

In chapter 'God given Talents and Gifts' we have learnt how important it is to be aware of our actions and how they impact others. But it leaves the big question: how will I possibly know what to do and how.

Is God really going to help me? What sort of help can I expect? It will not be an easy venture but as I pointed out in the very beginning of this chapter, life is fair, but certainly not easy.

Why not start at the beginning? In order to get any help from anyone, a rapport and relationship needs to be established first. Pray and tell God that you are ready to get to know Him. Ask Him into your heart. Every chapter in this book gives a glimpse of who God is and what kind of character He has. But a glimpse is only a glimpse. If you are still reading, I know that you are well on your way to learning more about God, which is what I'm praying for.

As I mentioned earlier on, forming a habit of reading some verses from the Bible everyday is a good place to begin. Then again, you would ask yourself where you should start reading. There are many Bible reading plans available online, which cover various topics to choose from. Some reading plans only go for a few days or a couple of weeks and others guide you through the entire Bible. You can pick the ones that are relevant for you now.

During one of the Alpha courses I prayed with my group. The topic we discussed was "How to have Faith" and why we need a relationship with God. As I started to pray with my eyes closed, big trees with prominent roots popped up in my mind. At first I thought that these images were a remnant of my walk in the park earlier. I was a bit confused as the same impression kept insisting in my mind. I couldn't work out what it all meant and how it fit into the context of Alpha. Suddenly I began to speak the following words:

> *"A relationship with God will strengthen you and drive your roots deeper into the soil of life."*

I was in awe. Nothing can measure up to God's wisdom. These are definitely not the kind of words I would express myself with.

A strong relationship with God draws you close to Him. You become to realise that you want God to be the most important part of your daily life. When you ask with the right intentions, God will help you in all areas of your life. All you need to do is trust and ask. God will guide and support you. As our Heavenly Father, He has your best interest at heart. His deepest desire is to have you as a part of His family. God said through His prophet Isaiah:

> *15 "Can a mother forget the baby at her breast*
> *and have no compassion on the child she has borne?*
> *Though she may forget,*
> *I will not forget you!*
> *16 See, I have engraved you on the palms of my hands;*
> *Isaiah 49:15 (NIV)*

He is our Father in Heaven and certainly knows what we need. His view from 'up there' is much greater than from the Eureka building in Melbourne (refer to Chapter "See God's View"). Last and but not least, He has been 'around for a while' to know best.

When you were a kid, did you ever worry where the money came from to pay for the mortgage? Did you even know that there was a mortgage? How about the family car, food, toys, school fees, music lessons, sport, clothes etc.? No, your parents took care of all of that. You trusted them and enjoyed your childhood, hanging out with your friends, playing sport and going to school. As we trusted our parents, so we ought to trust God as an adult. It's much easier to leave it all to God and let Him sit in the driver's seat. Let Him do the 'worrying'; if there ever really is anything to worry about. That gives you the space and freedom to enjoy a purposeful life. It frees your mind of unnecessary trepidations and fear just as it did during your childhood.

This is the kind of freedom that the apostle Paul is referring to in his letter to the Corinthian Church:

Now the LORD is the Spirit, and where the Spirit of the LORD is, there is freedom.
2 Corinthians 3:17 (NIV)

...and from the Old Testament:

Cast your cares on the LORD and he will sustain you; he will never let the righteous be shaken.
Psalm 55:22 (NIV)

As long as you follow what God intends for you, everything around you will fall into place. He will ensure that you will be equipped with all you need to succeed; finances, friends, contacts, ideas, energy, confidence and strength. Trust will require patience, as God's timing may not necessarily coincide with your own expectations.

Which points right back to the core of the apple…God, who sustains all our needs

I'll be right, God will provide

To follow God's ways actually leads us to freedom, freedom that is derived from trusting God with all our worries and concerns. The analogy in the Chapter titled "The Broom" sets up the perfect scene as an example.

God is the Creator and the only one who can see the complete picture; the past, present and the future. Time is of no consequence in the eternal realm where He resides. In so many passages in the Bible, Jesus tells us not to worry about the tomorrow. Only live in the moment and trust that God will provide us with exactly what we need abundantly, but not in a wasteful manner. If it happens to be too much for one's own use, then one is meant to share.

In most cases we are not in control. Never spend your time and energy on focusing on areas that you are not in control of. You cannot change other people and unforeseen events. Only focus on what you are in control of. You are always in control of your own thoughts, actions and reactions. When we pray, God will lead us. Then it is entirely up to us to trust and adhere to His guidance. The saying goes; *'you can lead a horse to the water, but you cannot make it drink'*. It is important to consider our actions very carefully. With God in your mind and heart you can grow into a confident and strong person. Why worry about something that most likely is not going to happen anyway; fear paralyses and keeps us captive. Fear and worries are not in congruence with personal progress and prosperity.

The following passages from the OT and NT outline that God provides for us daily, there is no need to hoard for the "rainy" days.

In the Gospel of Matthew, in the Sermon on the Mount, Jesus teaches us how to pray:

7 And when you pray, do not keep on babbling like pagans, for they think they will be heard because of their many words.
8 Do not be like them, for <u>your Father knows what you need before you ask him.</u>
9 "This, then, is how you should pray:

" 'Our Father in heaven,
hallowed be your name,
10 your kingdom come,
your will be done,
on Earth as it is in heaven.
11 Give us today our daily bread.
12 And forgive us our debts,
as we also have forgiven our debtors.
13 And lead us not into temptation,
but deliver us from the evil one. '
Matthew 6:8-13 (NIV)

We all have different needs; some need more, some less. Many times we believe that we require more than what we were given, until we realise that less was more than plenty. The book of 'Exodus' tells how God led the Jewish people out of Egypt and of slavery. It is great example of God's provision, guidance, protection and power. God sustained them with food and water for 40 years. He handed down clear instructions, which ensured their survival:

13 That evening quail came and covered the camp, and in the morning there was a layer of dew around the camp.
14 When the dew was gone, thin flakes like frost on the ground appeared on the desert floor.
15 When the Israelites saw it, they said to each other, "What is it?" For they did not know what it was. Moses said to them, "It is the bread the LORD has given you to eat.
16 This is what the LORD has commanded: 'Everyone is to gather as much as they need. Take an omer for each person you have in your tent.'"
17 The Israelites did as they were told; some gathered much,

some little. 18 And when they measured it by the omer, the one who gathered much did not have too much, and the one who gathered little did not have too little. Everyone had gathered just as much as they needed.
Exodus 16:13-18 (NIV)

The manna may no longer fall from the heavens, but God certainly delivers in many, sometimes unexpected and unique ways. It is a phenomenal feeling when God answers your prayers. Let me share with you a couple of instances when God responded to my prayers.

The first one: *In the early days when I began to write this book, I had concerns about not having sufficient time and energy alongside a full-time job and running my therapy business after hours. It turned out that I had no difficulties simplifying my life to allow for the necessary time, nor did my enthusiasm and commitment ever fade. If I did feel a bit tired after work, I took this as a sign to take a break.*

Last year I was called for jury duty. At the outset, I felt inconvenienced and also didn't feel quite so comfortable to judge another person. I prayed that if possible, I wouldn't be called in for a court case. Then I left this in God's hands and trusted Him that whichever way it was going to turn out that it would be beneficial to me. If I were to be selected as a juror, I would be able to experience an actual court case.

We were all waiting at the courthouse in the designated juror area. During the course of the day, they drew two ballots and my name never came up. I was so relieved and grateful. At the same time, I enjoyed a day off with educational insight in the legal system. I utilised the waiting hours working on the book. I made good progress that day and many unique ideas came my way. Amongst them was the picture of the apple. God had provided me with time and resources.

The second one: *Our church runs 3-4 Alpha courses per year.*

These are held on Monday nights. For many terms I have had the privilege to be part of the leadership team. We had a four month break after Christmas. This allowed me to allocate Monday evenings to work on my book. In April, we were to start a new term and I was hoping that I would not be required to participate, but at the same token, I didn't want to let the team down. So I prayed and asked God if there would be a chance that I may not be needed for this term in order to spend the time with writing. Otherwise, I would gladly volunteer for Alpha. I left whatever outcome in God's hands. I informed the church that if there were to be any new people who would like to step up, I would be more than happy to give this term a miss to free up my time.

At the meeting that followed, the roles were being discussed and people were selected. I was not amongst them. Part of me was so pleased with this positive outcome (thank you Lord), but the other part of me was a bit disappointed. I guess my ego got a bit dinted. This incident led me to understand that following God's Will can sometimes cause some hurt, but it helps us grow spiritually. However, it was a very 'small pain' with very great gain. This experience has taught me a big lesson. It pays to keep a check on my haughty attitude and become a bit humble. Is this not mentioned in the Bible too…?

In the Old Testament:
> For the LORD takes delight in his people;
> he crowns the humble with victory.
> Psalm 149:4 (NIV)

…and the New Testament:
> But he gives us more grace. That is why Scripture says:
> "God opposes the proud
> but shows favor to the humble."
> James 4:6 (NIV)

If there is *receiving* there also must be *giving*. There are the less fortunate, people who are, for various reasons unable to support themselves. This is when *giving* comes into play. The Bible uses the word **tithing**, which means 10% of what you earn.

Here is what the English dictionary says:

tithe |tīTH|
noun
one tenth of annual produce or earnings, formerly taken as a tax for the support of the church and clergy.
(in certain religious denominations) a tenth of an individual's income pledged to the church.

ORIGIN: Old English tēotha (adjective in the ordinal sense 'tenth,' used in a specialized sense as a noun), tēothian (verb).

... and here is what God says in the Old Testament

30" 'A tithe of everything from the land, whether grain from the soil or fruit from the trees, belongs to the LORD; it is holy to the LORD
Leviticus 27:30 (NIV)

Bring the whole tithe into the storehouse, that there may be food in my house. Test me in this," says the LORD Almighty, "and see if I will not throw open the floodgates of heaven and pour out so much blessing that there will not be room enough to store
Malachi 3:10 (NIV)

...and in the New Testament, Paul speaks of sharing the 'income' with others as well as look after people who give spiritual support, meaning working in the name of the Lord, supporting and teaching others:

10 Yes, this was written for us, because whoever plows and threshes should be able to do so in the hope of sharing in the

11 If we have sown spiritual seed among you, is it too much if
we reap a material harvest from you?
1 Corinthians 9:10-11 (NIV)

Have you ever wondered on what God based the 10%? Why is it not 12% or 9.25%? Being God, He already had the foresight of how the future will unfold. Looking at today's population, the entire world's wealth is divided into 90% of 'average' to very poor people as opposed to 10% of people who are wealthy. Within this 90% I would estimate that 50% are struggling to even survive.

Can you see how the calculation works out? Unfortunately, not all who fit into the 10% echelon are sharing their 10% income. If this were the case, no one would go hungry. This would make up for the lesser income groups who either can't afford or don't dare to donate 10% of their small income. The tithing could sustain various charity organisations that take care of people who are in dire need, affected by natural disasters, sickness, war or premature death.

I have calculated another formula that could work: what if everybody in the world who earns any kind of income, from a business, a job, a pension or any other compensational payouts, would give only one Dollar (or equivalent to the buying power of their currency) per fortnight? Our world would be a different place, no poverty, homelessness, starvation, lack of medical care, education, sanitation or water. Would there still be grounds for crime and wars? Dream on… but it is worth a thought.

On the upside, so many people contribute above the 10%. Others give up their time and volunteer to help the less fortunate. They realise that by sharing their blessings, they not only feel gratified, but also become rich in spirit by blessing others. For some people it is easier to give than to take and to say yes than no.

Jesus says:

"It is easier for a camel to go through the eye of a needle than for someone who is rich to enter the kingdom of God."
Mark 10:25 (NIV)

Jesus knows human nature. Are we this greedy? What makes us be this way? Alas, most people hang on to what they have, scared that they may not have enough. Their income by far succeeds their needs. They are compelled to save for the 'rainy days' that may never even eventuate.

A while back when finances where a bit tight, I got quite worried as how I could manage to meet my financial commitments. Aloud I said to myself: *"I'll be right, God will provide."* To my surprise, I instantly felt relieved and even liked the way it rhymed. Try it someday; it will make you feel better too.

One needs to trust and have faith to let go of financial worries. Trust that God will provide for your needs. Share your surplus with others who are in a strife. It only takes a very small portion of your income but it can make a life changing difference to someone else. It will come back in a hundred fold. God always keeps His promises:

Four years ago, things were quite tough. The interest rates were high and I had to watch the dollar to make ends meet. One Sunday at church, the collection bucket came my way and I opened my purse looking for some money to give. There was no change, only a 'big' note. My very first thought was that I couldn't afford to give that much. Then I shrugged my shoulders and I asked myself, why not? There are people out there who need it more than I do. I placed the note in the bucket and it made me feel good.

I moved on and totally forgot about it. Not long after God surprised me, it returned to me, with interest. I remember thinking: Wow, it really works! On another occasion when money got scarce, I asked God to 'replenish' my coffers and to my utter surprise, it happened just 5 minutes after I asked. I didn't even pray as such; I only looked up to the sky and one sentence was all it took.

God rewards you in different ways when you care for others. We are all children of God, therefore brothers and sisters. Who could turn their backs on their own sibling? It does not always happen so quickly. Never place any specific expectations as God has His own timetable.

Instead of feeling troubled,
fill your heart with joy and sing

Instead of worrying about yourself,
make someone else smile

Instead of holding on,
pass it on

Monica

Jesus tells us tells (*King refers to Jesus*):

34 "Then the King will say to those on his right, 'Come, you who are blessed by my Father; take your inheritance, the kingdom prepared for you since the Creation of the world.
35 For I was hungry and you gave me something to eat, I was thirsty and you gave me something to drink, I was a stranger and you invited me in,
36 I needed clothes and you clothed me, I was sick and you looked after me, I was in prison and you came to visit me.'
Matthew 25:34-36 (NIV)

Always keep in mind that God is everywhere and in each one of us; we are all one. God never forgets anyone, so let us not forget our fellowman.

Which points right back to the core of the apple…God, who blesses us to be a blessing to others

Why the Bible?

What is the Bible?

I have briefly touched on the Bible in the first chapter (Foreword) and in many other chapters I pointed out how important it is to pick up the Bible on a daily basis. Nevertheless, when someone recommends a book to us, naturally we want to find out more before we will decide to read it. By this time, you would have already read quite a few passages as you worked through the various chapters.

The Bible would be the most talked about and read books of all times, translated in over 531 languages. Merely looking at the English translation, it comes in almost 900 different versions of which not all are complete. Most of the verses I quoted in this book are from the New International Version (NIV). The NIV is one of the more popular English versions and easy to understand.

Bible is a Hebrew word, meaning **Library**. It contains a collection of 66 books written by about 44 authors, divided in 2 sections: the Old Testament and the New Testament. To give you an overview of the complete Bible, I have listed all the books according to the type of message and objective:

1. The Old Testament Books

We need to read the Old Testament as a lead up to the New Testament, it all points to Jesus. God is telling us that He is the God of all nations, not just for the Israelites. The OT Books are categorised as:

The Pentateuch
- Genesis
- Exodus
- Leviticus
- Numbers
- Deuteronomy

Historical Books
- Joshua
- Judges
- Ruth
- 1 Samuel
- 2 Samuel
- 1 Kings
- 2 Kings
- 1 Chronicles
- 2 Chronicles
- Ezra
- Nehemiah
- Esther

Wisdom Literature
- Job
- Psalms
- Proverbs
- Ecclesiastes
- Song of Solomon

Major Prophets
- Isaiah
- Jeremiah
- Lamentations
- Ezekiel
- Daniel

Minor Prophets

- Hosea
- Joel
- Amos
- Obadiah
- Jonah
- Micah
- Nahum
- Habakkuk
- Zephaniah
- Haggai
- Zechariah
- Malachi

2. The New Testament Books

The New Testament opens up with the four *Gospels* (= the Good News) written by Matthew, Mark, Luke and John. The dictionary says:

noun

*1 (**the Gospel**) the Gospel according to John: Christian teaching, Christian doctrine, Christ's teaching; the word of God, the good news, the New Testament.*

2 don't treat this as Gospel: the truth; fact, actual fact, reality, actuality, factuality, the case, a certainty.

The Gospels

Matthew: The Gospel of Matthew presents undeniable evidence that Jesus Christ is the promised Saviour, the Messiah.

Mark: The Gospel of Mark illustrates who Jesus Christ is as a person.

Luke: The Gospel of Luke reveals the humanity of Jesus Christ.

John: The Gospel of John reveals Jesus as the Son of God.

The four **Gospels** convey hope and truth to all nations. They are testimonies of eyewitnesses who knew Jesus personally. Their account begins with the genealogy, the lead up to the birth and resurrection of Jesus and ends with His ascension. The apostles proclaim the promise and hope of salvation to the world through Jesus. They pass on His teachings and tell us that we can all be part of God's family. We could also describe the Gospels as the climax of the whole Bible. The Gospels tell us of a Hero named Jesus, who prevails and triumphs over death, concluded by "happily ever after". The *Good News* is that we too can gain salvation and eternal life through Jesus Christ, the Son of God.

Historical Books

The Book of Acts: In the book of Acts, the apostle Luke recounts the immediate development of the Early Church after the resurrection of Jesus. It tells how the apostles received the gifts of the Holy Spirit at the day of Pentecost, followed by evangelism and discipleship of other nations.

From there, the New Testament continues on with the **Epistles**, which are letters written by the apostles to the early churches. Their purpose was to guide believers and lead new people to Jesus and His promise of hope and eternal life. It was of upmost importance to the apostles that the teaching remained unchanged and authentic to what Jesus was teaching. There were many false teachers who tried to lead new believers astray. The Epistles are filled with amazing insights of how to live a worthy life, making a difference and warnings of the consequences of walking on the wrong path.

Pauline Epistles

Romans: God's plan of salvation by the faith in Jesus Christ.

1Corinthians: Outlines why the apostle Paul wrote such an uncompromising letter to the young Christians in Corinth. This city was saturated with corruption and idolatry. This new church was troubled with questions and had serious problems of division, sexual immorality and disorderly conduct.

2Corinthians: This book talks about the personal relationship between a pastor (the apostle Paul) and his church. Paul encountered painful opposition to his authority by a false teacher in Corinth.

Galatians: The letter to the Galatian church outlines that we are not saved by obeying the Law but by faith in Jesus Christ as Savior. The Jewish Christians learned how they gained freedom from the burden of Moses law.

Ephesians: Paul gives the Ephesian church practical and encouraging advice on how to live a life that honors God. The book of Ephesians is very relevant in today's conflict-ridden world.

Philippians: The book of Philippians talks about the secret to being content in every situation. Paul teaches us how we can still have joy in the midst of turbulent and challenging times.

Colossians: Here Paul expands on the characteristics of a true Christian and how we need to grow in our spiritual life.

1Thessalonians: Paul encourages and teaches the Thessalonians how, as new Christians, to stay true to their faith in any circumstances.

2Thessalonians: It continues on from 1Thessalonians, Paul clears up the misconceptions about when Jesus will return.

1Timothy: In this book to Timothy, Paul's gives clear instructions for us and passes on specific rules for godly behaviour.

2Timothy Here Paul writes how to choose competent church leaders and the qualities expected of them to be up to such a responsible task. He also touches on forgiveness and equality.

General Epistles

Hebrews: The author of this book has not been able to be established. There are many speculations. It is addressed to the Hebrew Christians who were wavering in their faith.

James: James was the brother of Jesus. Here James provides practical advice for Christians. It only has 3 chapters but it is packed with advice that is very relevant to us now.

1Peter
2Peter
1John
2John
3John
Jude

Apocalyptic Literature

Revelation: The last book of the Bible, written by the apostle John. He describes the explosive clash between the Kingdom of God and evil. It is composed in an apocalyptic writing style in form of numeric and visual metaphors and representations. The word *apocalyptic* originates from the Greek: uncover. It is very symbolic, therefore can be rather difficult to understand. One needs to be familiar with certain symbols and references that can be found throughout the whole Bible.

Indeed, the Bible is no ordinary book. It is also rather fascinating to hear how famous people have described the Bible:

"The Gospel is not a book; it is a living being, with an action, a power, which invades everything that opposes its extension, behold! It is upon this table: This book, surpassing all others. I never omit to read it, and every day with some pleasure."
Napoleon Bonaparte, Emperor of the French (from 1804-1814), 1769-1821

"We account the Scriptures of God to be the most sublime philosophy. I find more sure marks of authenticity in the Bible than in any profane history whatsoever."
Isaac Newton, English mathematician and scientist, 1642-1727

"I am busily engaged in the study of the Bible. I believe it is God's word because it finds me where I am."
"I believe the Bible is the best gift God has ever given to man. All the good of the Saviour of the world is communicated to us through the Book."
Abraham Lincoln, 16th President of the United States, 1809-1865

"You Christians look after a document containing enough dynamite to blow all civilisation to pieces, turn the world upside down and bring peace to a battle-torn planet. But you treat it as though it is nothing more than a piece of literature."
Mahatma Gandhi, lawyer, leader and advocate and of India's independence movement, 1869-1948

For a number of years I intended to read the whole Bible. I was so curious to discover its secrets, yet I was filled with doubts. What kept me from reading the Bible for so long was that of its authenticity. Another concern was how and where I would begin to read. How could I trust a book that has been translated so many times during thousands of years? Being re-written by different people, would it not have lost its true essence? Surely, what we read today, wouldn't it significantly deviate from the original scrolls?

Many other questions circled around my mind. Why is there so much prominence put onto the Bible? Are these Scriptures genuine? Would they not be outdated? How can these ancient scrolls still influence us today? Is the Bible more than a history book? Are these really God's words speaking to us through the Bible? I was fascinated to learn that all translations are accurate and literally unchanged from the original scrolls. The last book of the New Testament puts it this way:

18 I warn everyone who hears the words of the prophecy of this scroll: If anyone adds anything to them, God will add to that person the plagues described in this scroll.
19 And if anyone takes words away from this scroll of prophecy, God will take away from that person any share in the tree of life and in the Holy City, which are described in this scroll.
Revelation 22:18-19 (NIV)

With this kind of warning, would anyone really dare to make any changes…?

A few years back, I received a phone call that my mother had to go to hospital. It was not life threatening but I still wanted to fly back to Switzerland to be with her. She had already been suffering from Multiple Sclerosis for several years. She was so happy that I came and proudly introduced me to everyone at the hospital. Everyday we spent time together, talking, sharing and just enjoying each other's company. Despite her being in hospital, we spent a wonderful time together. Probably these were one of the closest moments with my mum in my adult years.

One day, when we sat in the cafeteria over a cup of coffee and cake, we ran into our 'old' priest from our village. He had retired from there a few years back and was now working at the hospital to minister to the sick and dying.

He was delighted to see us and joined us for a chat. I thought that he was in fact a rather nice man. You need to know though, as kids, we used to make fun of him, especially about his driving skills. His motto was, 'I drive and you watch out'. We were always making jokes about him. We once watched him backing up his car to park on the school ground. In the process though, he 'ran' over a small tree and didn't even seem to notice. You can imagine how we were laughing our heads off. Yes, as kids we had a different perspective. However, sitting there with him at the table, I felt sorry, especially that we never took time to understand and appreciate him enough.

Finally, I had the opportunity to ask him a question that had been on my mind for a very long time; I wanted to find out why we never read the Bible at school. At first he looked at me with a startled expression on his face but then answered my question. He explained that the Bible could not just be read like a 'normal' book, its content can be interpreted in too many different ways. It would have been too complex to expound. Therefore, the reading of the Bible was not part of the curriculum.

When I started to go to church, I joined one of the many lifegroups (also referred to as life cells). These are small groups that meet up to study the Bible and pray together. Slowly I began to read the Bible in the company my experienced friends. I brought up all my questions to find out what their thoughts were. I soon started to understand what the Bible really is. The Bible is a 'living' Book that is filled with the Spirit of God. God speaks to us through the Holy Scriptures and answers with verses that can speak directly into a specific area in which one is struggling. Wisdom and guidance is revealed to a person who seeks and wants to learn with the right mindset.

Others dismiss the Bible as being only a history book.

Quite the contrary; the Bible is a book with a purpose. The Old Testament points towards the salvation of Jesus. The historical Books, mainly in the Old Testament bring history into play as a vehicle to illustrate the consequences of actions and reactions. People can relate much easier to accounts of real events. Stories are much more effective than reading some textbook theories.

For everything that was written in the past was written to teach us, so that through the endurance taught in the Scriptures and the encouragement they provide we might have hope.
Romans 15:4 (NIV)

No matter how many times we read the whole Bible, we will never cease to learn. Endlessly, new wisdom is being revealed. No one has ever been able to claim that they had completed the study of the Bible. The Bible is a never-ending book, designed for us to grow in our never-ending spiritual life. Like God, it has no end. The same chapters and verses can be read over and over again. Each time it will transform into a different meaning, befitting the level of one's personal growth and understanding.

In fact, the more you learn and advance, the more you get to know the character of God and what He intends for you. The more we know, the more we realise just how much more there is to learn.

The Bible accompanies us on our journey of discovering what life and God is all about. The Scriptures continuously open up new horizons that forge newer and bigger visions, the sort of visions that only God can impart. The Bible definitely is alive with the Spirit of God. For this very reason, it is beyond comparison.

The Old Testament deals with a wealth of history in which God reveals Himself by miraculous events, making a covenant and showing His love and desire for us. Through His chosen prophets, He instructs people and unveils great things to come. The Old Testament is a preparation and lead up to the New Testament. It is packed with prophecies and revelations that point to the birth of Jesus, His life, death and resurrection.

Many consider the Old and New Testament to be two separate books of the Holy Bible, but in fact, it is one Book. In other words, we could call it 'The Bible - Part I&2'.

We also need to bear in mind that some of the stories in the OT are metaphorical. The accounts of the Israelites distinctly relate to our very own circumstances today. It makes it evident that history certainly seems to repeat itself over and over again, anywhere in the world.

What are the messages telling and teaching us today? Looking at the Bible in this light you may understand its true purpose and how important it will become in your life.

It highlights the kind of life we need to strive for. We can apply the Bible as our development book as it speaks into all aspects of life. The Bible is God's way of talking to each one of us at our very own personal level of growth and awareness. God meets us where we are and reveals as much as we need to know to grow or to overcome challenges.

In the chapter "*Why not sin*" I have outlined each of the Ten Commandments. You will discover that they still apply to us today. We can look at the Bible and its purpose in many other ways. When I was contemplating how to best portray the Bible, a few ideas came to mind. The first one was:

The User Manual

How many times would you have asked yourself these or similar questions:

- What am I supposed to do with my life?
- Why am I not succeeding?
- Where and why do I go wrong?
- How do I interact with other people?
- What can I and what can't I do?
- Where am I supposed to be in life?
- Which one is the right decision?
- …Why, what, how, who….?

Don't you wish you were given a personal user manual when you were born? Wouldn't this be much easier? Whenever you would get stuck, you could just look up the instructions.

Why then don't we contact <u>our</u> manufacturer and ask for a user manual? Maybe we don't know where and how to contact the manufacturer. Is it *God@god.com* or could we perhaps find it on *www.god.com*? One would wish it was that easy… and it is, but just a little bit different. That is why you are holding this book in your hands.

God IS the manufacturer and knows exactly how we are meant to function. Therefore, he made sure to give as a User Manual. Yes, you are in fact born with a user manual, the Bible.

A few years ago I bought this fantastic computer (I won't mention the name) but never looked up the instructions. I only make use of what I know or can work out myself. This leaves a huge percentage of its functionality untapped. The same applies to us humans. We only ever get to access a small portion of our full capacity, although God encoded us with a programme that would enable us to reach our full potential. Yet we do not take heed of the manufacturer's manual.

Jesus answered, "It is written: 'Man shall not live on bread alone, but on every word that comes from the mouth of God.' "
Matthew 4:4 (NIV)

Because we are the pinnacle of God's Creation, we are designed to fulfill our purpose in life. The Bible is our User Manual and equips us to master any of the challenges we face in life. We could also refer to the Bible as a Self Development Book on *'How to obtain a healthy lifestyle', 'How to live a prosperous life', 'How to apply psychology', 'How to overcome testing times', 'How to lead a meaningful life', 'How to make friends'* and so forth.

In its entirety, the Bible covers all three aspects, the trinity of Body – Mind – Spirit.

God ensures that we can maintain physical as well as mental health by living by the right values. Because the words are His Words, the Bible too is a lifelong manual with no expiry date.

All Scripture is God-breathed and is useful for teaching, rebuking, correcting and training in righteousness,
2 Timothy 3:16 (NIV)

It is an amazing journey to explore and probe the deeper levels of God's wisdom. You will find answers to a particular question or receive guidance to resolve an issue. The Bible will calm your mind in the midst of life's torrents.

Which points right back to the core of the apple…God, our Mentor

Panasonic or Sony?

I am sure you would be wondering how *Panasonic* could possibly relate to the Bible or to 'exploring the big questions of life'. These days, more and more people get so lost in this crazy world, filled to the brim with news of wars, stock-market crashes, crime, unemployment, global conflicts and natural disasters. This all affects us in our personal and family life. Amidst a kaleidoscope of wild images, we try to find our way in search of answers to our questions.

Are you looking in the right places? Are you asking the right people? What are we supposed to do and where do we go when we have reached the end of the road and break down? Will we visit the local doctor and get some anti-depressants or other 'fix-it-all' drugs?

Let me ask you another question. What would you do if your expensive Panasonic TV would break down? Of course, you would try everything possible to get it working. If all fails, who would you contact for help? Would you pack up your TV and go to Sony to get it fixed? Could they be of assistance with parts and repairs? I am convinced though that you would take your Panasonic TV directly to PANASONIC. Why? The answer is very simple; Panasonic is the manufacturer and has designed and built your TV. They will instantly know what has caused the malfunction and are able to repair your TV with the original parts. Panasonic knows its own products intimately.

So, why is it, that, when people 'break down' they seek a Psychiatrist, Psychologist or Counselor? For some strange reason, we are running around, desperately looking for a genius who can 'fix' us. We spend hundreds of dollars on seminars, workshops, books, DVD's or CD's just to find a way to get back on our feet.

Are you a Panasonic or a Sony? Who made you? Who created and designed you? Who has given you the breath of life? Who has lovingly bestowed your special abilities upon you that set you apart from all the others? Who is always looking out for you, loves you unconditionally and forgives you for whatever you may have done? Is this not your God? HE is your manufacturer. HE knows exactly how you function and He has all the original parts. There is no one else who knows you better. He perfectly understands your pain and anguish; knows all your needs and desires.

6 Are not five sparrows sold for two pennies? Yet not one of them is forgotten by God.
7 Indeed, the very hairs of your head are all numbered. Don't be afraid; you are worth more than many sparrows.
Luke 12:6-7 (NIV)

If God does not forget a sparrow, then how much more will He remember you? How much more are you worth to Him? You are His Creation and He knows you intimately, even down to your every hair.

So why don't we turn to our Maker in the first place? Why don't we go and ask God? Is it that we don't know Him or is it that we may even be afraid of Him? Could it be that we feel unworthy or not good enough in God's eyes? Are we uncertain that He can even hear us? Why is it that some of us only resort to God when we are at the end of our tether? At the point where we have exhausted all avenues and found no solutions? Sadly, some people will never turn to God, even when they arrived at the end of the road.

God has created us with a free will. What exactly does this mean? I have referred to our *free will* on quite a number of occasions. Not without a reason because I believe this is such a pivotal point. It is mostly overlooked, misunderstood or not being paid enough importance to. With the free will in place, how then can we possibly expect God to just 'butt in' whenever He sees that one of us is in some sort of a strive? By doing so, would He not cross the line and go against His own principles and promises?

God never changes and does not go against our free will. It seems obvious that we are not ready for His help. It is up to us to take the initiative and approach God for help just as we would take our broken down Panasonic to Panasonic. God is very patient and has all the time in eternity to wait for us. We must take responsibility for ourselves and get into action. The sooner we do the better for us.

Even to your old age and gray hairs
I am he, I am he who will sustain you.
I have made you and I will carry you;
I will sustain you and I will rescue you.
Isaiah 46:4 (NIV)

Is it not comforting to know that God is always close by to step in when we are in need of His help and strength? Just like any manufacturer, He has a well equipped workshop.

Which points right back to the core of the apple…God, who knows each one of us intimately

The "Never-Ending Story"

And here is my final interpretation of the Holy Scriptures, this time in form of a picture. The longer I have been reading the Bible, the more I came to realise that indeed, it is a never-ending Book; the Never-Ending Story of a Creation that promises an Everlasting Life.

God reveals His wisdom tailor-made to each individual reader. We all come from different backgrounds with a different upbringing, culture, viewpoint and experiences. Some may have been reading and studying the Bible for a number of years, some have just begun and others never even opened a Bible. So the level of growth of each person differs.

During a Bible study at church, a sudden vision of the Bible appeared in my mind. The Bible is not a 'flat' textbook but it releases knowledge and wisdom in various layers. Wisdom is gradually unveiled within each layer that contains the precise message the reader is seeking and ready for.

It all begins with the top layer. As the understanding and the love for God grows within a person, it progresses to the next level. God will open the person's eyes and heart to understand the deeper strata that follow.

It is a never-ending and very exciting journey to unwrap God's secrets. The more we grow in faith, the more we feel God in our life, the more we trust, the further we step back and let God lead the way. We become less concerned about the worldly stuff and turn our focus toward our spiritual needs. Furthermore, we will be capable to comprehend the true essence of the Holy Scriptures.

In my vision, each layer represented a door that opens up as one begins to discover the inspirations, directions, foresights, wisdom and prophecies that God conveys through His chosen authors. I believe there will come a time when there is no need for any words, as complete comprehension will have entered the consciousness. As I sat there in wonder, I saw how the final door opened and before me appeared the whole universe with its billions of stars and galaxies. It was a breathtaking yet, metaphorical picture. When we close our eyes for good, only then will we be capable to open the final door and 'see' the whole truth.

The Bible is the portal that holds the coordinates to eternal life. We cannot just read the Bible within our own wisdom; we need a key to unlock it. Jesus is the One who holds that key. Whoever believes in Him will be given the ability to understand through His Holy Spirit. I noticed that in many passages a particular writer would only release a fraction of what he actually was shown by God. These insights are easily missed, but when you spot them, I promise you will get goose bumps. They wrote with such conviction and faith that I truly believe God had opened the final gateway to them; they saw the ultimate truth. How hard would it have been to describe such revelations in words? That is why we find so many repetitions in the Bible, expressed in such diverse interpretations.

The apostles were the first to impart and pass on the revolutionary teachings of Jesus. What a tremendous responsibility that God had laid upon them. They relentlessly continued with their task and never gave up teaching the 'Good News' and leading the early churches. With a clarity that only God could have revealed to them, they knew it was worth everything they had.

I believe that Moses caught a glimpse through that last door, aka stratum. It was even visible to the people of Israel. Moses had spent forty days and nights in the presence of God on Mount Sinai:

29 When Moses came down from Mount Sinai with the two tablets of the covenant law in his hands, he was not aware that his face was radiant because he had spoken with the LORD.
30 When Aaron and all the Israelites saw Moses, his face was radiant, and they were afraid to come near him.

and

35 they saw that <u>his face was radiant</u>. Then <u>Moses would put the veil back over his face</u> until he went in to speak with the LORD.
Exodus 39:29-30 & 35 (NIV)

Which points right back to the core of the apple…God, who is the ultimate Truth

Footnote:

This is what happened to me. It all began when I started to receive insightful thoughts or perhaps we could call them also 'messages' or 'bright moments'. It usually happened during church services, Bible studies, in the car or walking. I was worried that I would forget so I started my 'God Diary'. Then, many months later, I felt a profound prompting to write a book. Soon after, my friend at Alpha introduced me to the BiOY (Bible in One Year) app. I loved the idea of reading the whole bible in a guided format. I commenced with the programme at the start of the following year. To my surprise, I continuously found Bible verses that would match up with my insights. And so it all started unfold. There were many instances when I literally saw certain verses highlighted. Each time I found passages that stood out, I felt God reaffirmed that what I was writing is what He wanted convey. It gave me the confidence and perseverance to continue with my work. It is phenomenal how revealing the Bible is.

Epilogue

~   The End   ~

…and a New Beginning

Now that you have arrived at *the End*, the final chapter of **WHY,** you may ask yourself **WHAT** is next. Do you feel that a new door is opening for you? Can you see life in a different light? Have some the questions been answered for you? Has it raised new and deeper questions? Do you want to continue and learn more? There are a host of choices available to you. The best will be the one that feels right for you.

First and foremost, it is important that you get connected. I'm taking the liberty of suggesting a couple of ideas that can assist you on your journey to a new beginning; a life being transformed by Jesus in such ways that you cannot possibly imagine.

- You may want to find a *local church* and connect with people. Many churches host various **courses** to learn more about yourself, life and God. It doesn't really matter what Christian denomination it is, all of them follow the teachings of Jesus. Churches have their own individual cultures and traditions. You may want to pop into a church or two and find the one that you are most comfortable with. Christians are nice and forthcoming and easy to connect with. It is important though to be connected with a Christian community.

- I found *Alpha* very helpful, providing a safe and unthreatening environment. Alpha consists of a series of interactive sessions that explore the basics of the Christian faith. There are normally 3-4 Alpha terms held yearly at various locations in many parts of the world per. You can find available courses in your area on the Internet, which makes it very easy to plan ahead. The courses are held free of charge because God should be accessible and available to everyone.

- In a few of the chapters I have touched on how vital it is to read the **Bible**. Nowadays, there are free **Bible Apps** that you can download on your phone, tablet or computer. Alongside they have a variety of Bible reading plans available. It makes reading the Bible so much easier. They can go from a few days up to a year and have a variety of topics to choose from. You may also find someone that would like to read the Bible with you, which is so much more fun. Some churches have **Life Groups** also known as **Life Cells**. Who knows, there may be a group that would suit you. There are so many ways how we can read a Bible. As it so happens, you have already started to read the Bible. 'WHY – Us against God' has taken you on an introductory tour around the World of the Holy Scripture.

- Perhaps this book has inspired you to look out for other **Books** to read; maybe watch Bible stories on **DVD**'s. Or a family member or a friend is happy to lend you a book and give you t endless. You can download countless **e-books** and **audio books** from Online Bookstores sites.

- As we have entered the Internet era, it has opened up numerous possibilities for you to connect with **online church services, podcasts of teachings and sermons, Christian worship music, online Life Groups** and many other **Christian Communities.** The Internet is your oyster, go, surf the big waves and find your precious Pearl.

What comes after 'WHAT'?

There is a **NEXT** after **WHAT**. It is an 'A New Beginning'. Jesus refers to it as the *Great Commission*. It simply means sharing the Good News with others:

19 Therefore go and make disciples of all nations, baptizing them in the name of the Father and of the Son and of the Holy Spirit,
20 and teaching them to obey everything I have commanded you. And surely I am with you always, to the very end of the age."
Matthew 28:19-20 (NIV)

and:

Again Jesus said, "Peace be with you! As the Father has sent me, I am sending you."
John 20:21 (NIV)

It is up to us, who already understand the truth to go out and share with others. Jesus tells us that He will return once the whole world **knows** His name. This does not mean that everyone has to nor will everyone believe in His name. But the name of Jesus and His promise must have reached all the corners of the Earth. *First, we were the Harvest and now it is us who are the workers.* We need to harvest the fruit that God has sown since the beginning:

The Harvest

36 When he (Jesus) saw the crowds, he had compassion on them, because they were harassed and helpless, like sheep without a shepherd.

37 Then he said to his disciples, "The harvest is plentiful but the workers are few.
38 Ask the LORD of the harvest, therefore, to send out workers into his harvest field."
Matthew 9:36-38 (NIV)

and:

37 "All those the Father gives me will come to me, and whoever comes to me I will never drive away."

39 " And this is the will of him who sent me, that I shall lose none of all those he has given me, but raise them up at the last day."

44 "No one can come to me unless the Father who sent me draws them, and I will raise them up at the last day."
John 6:37, 39, 44 (NIV)

During the **Kairos Course** at church, as we looked at the following verses, I began to see a deeper meaning that relates to us now. I have added my own comments in *italic*. This is what Jesus said to His disciples:

7 "As you go, proclaim this message: 'The kingdom of heaven has come near.'
8 Heal the sick, raise the dead, cleanse those who have leprosy, drive out demons. Freely you have received; freely give."
Matthew 10:7-8 (NIV)

The kingdom of heaven is near: *God is closer than you may think. He is accessible to everyone.*

Heal all the sick: *By sharing, we can heal the souls of people and give them hope in the name of Jesus. God is pure love and no evil (sickness) can exist in the presence of pure love.*

Raise the dead: *find and share with the ones who are lost to drugs and other addictions, victims of crime and people groups that have not yet been reached.*

Cleanse those who have leprosy: *tell people about God's ways, pass on the teachings of Jesus so that they too may learn of the consequences of sin. Show them how to forgive and love others.*

Drive out the demons: *withstand all temptations of evil, stand up for yourself and others; help others and don't allow evil to gain ANY foothold.*

Freely you receive, freely you must give: *God's love is a free gift to all and sets the standard of how we should treat others. We need to share the love of God.*

The 'Good News' can also travel fast. If we can tell others about a great new movie that had just been released or a terrific new restaurant around the corner, I think that sharing hope with others is a natural thing to do. Anyone who has been touched by God gets excited. Having one's life changed by 180 degrees, who wouldn't want but tell others about their experience? We cannot allow others to miss out. Moreover, how can anyone possibly keep the most sought after secret to himself or herself? When I see people doing it tough, I just want to tell them my story and show them how God can turn it all around for them too. Unfortunately, the timing may not always be appropriate, but I love to share the hope with others whenever possible. To start a conversation is not as hard as we may think.

27 What I tell you in the dark, speak in the daylight; what is
whispered in your ear, proclaim from the roofs.
28 Do not be afraid of those who kill the body but cannot kill
the soul. Rather, be afraid of the One who can destroy both
soul and body in hell.
Matthew 10:27-28 (NIV)

We may often try to talk about God and the common response is: No, I'm not interested in religion. Then we get stuck and tongue tied. I respond by saying that Jesus is not a religion. He has come to this world to teach us and not to condemn us. If you would like to get to know who Jesus really is and learn about His character, begin with the 4 Gospels of Matthew, Mark, Luke and John.

In the Old Testament, the passages of the prophet Amos clearly outline that even God doesn't want religion. What He desires is that we conduct ourselves in upright ways:

21 "I hate, I despise your religious festivals;
your assemblies are a stench to me.
22 Even though you bring me burnt offerings and grain
offerings,
I will not accept them.
Though you bring choice fellowship offerings,
I will have no regard for them.
23 Away with the noise of your songs!
I will not listen to the music of your harps.
*24 **But let justice roll on like a river,***
righteousness like a never-failing stream!
Amos 5:21-24 (NIV)

Or the version of The Message (MSG) says it this way:

21-24 "I can't stand your religious meetings.
I'm fed up with your conferences and conventions.
I want nothing to do with your religion projects,
your pretentious slogans and goals.
I'm sick of your fund-raising schemes,

your public relations and image making.
I've had all I can take of your noisy ego-music.
When was the last time you sang to me?
Do you know what I want?
I want justice—oceans of it.
I want fairness—rivers of it.
That's what I want.
That's all I want.
Amos 5:21-24 (MSG)

And this is my own version and it goes like this: "God is sitting on His Throne and pounding His fist on the table (if there is such a thing as a 'heavenly' table…?), shouting:

1 "Don't you guys get it?!! I am not a religion!
2 It is so simple; I don't need all the frilly bits,
3 I don't need all your manmade traditions and pretence,
4 I just want YOU! I want what is in your heart.
5 All I'm interested in is that you follow my word
6 Open your eyes and wake up!!"
Monica's version 1:1-6

Isn't this straight forward? Religion is man made, not God made. Why is it that we have all these various religions making it complicated? It gives rise to so much friction and can even lead to fanaticism. There are so many different Christian denominations: Eastern & Oriental Orthodox, Baptists, Catholics, Anglicans, Lutherans, Protestants and many others.

Aren't we all **<u>Christians </u>= Faith in Christ = Follower of Jesus Christ = Christ-ians?**

Today (26.10.14), when I left church, I past a young man sitting outside, studying his Bible. He had used a highlighter to assist him in his reading. It touched my heart to see a young person reading the Bible. I pray that more and more young people will believe in the power of the Bible.

As I kept walking, I remembered how I was wrestling earlier this year. As I started my journey with "Bible in One Year – BiOY" programme, I had become increasingly fascinated and wanted to extend my studies further. I was leaning towards the idea of enrolling in a Bible college or acquiring a theological degree. I admire the pastors at my church for their in depth knowledge of the Scriptures. I aspired to be just like them. I felt I needed to know much more before I could lead people to faith. After a few days of reflection and pondering, I stopped and became aware of what I was trying to procrastinate.

I realised that all I needed was faith, to know and understand God and the willingness to follow Him. It is as simple as that, without any 'frills'. To tell others about Jesus does not require a theological degree, it 'only' requires faith and the desire and passion to follow Him in anyway that He needs us to.

On the other hand, a theological degree does not necessarily require faith, it only requires the student to be interested in learning, to turn up, study and complete the course. So, what is really important here? Is it faith or knowledge? I put the idea of studying on ice. I felt that all I needed to do for now was to focus on completing this book and to continue with my voluntary activities at my church. As I was approaching my car, I felt that God was reaffirming my thoughts.

People get all excited and get stuck into learning and perfecting themselves. God doesn't want our main activity to be reading and studying the Bible. He wants us to read it on a daily basis but also to be proactive. Faith without action does not accomplish anything.

17 In the same way, faith by itself, if it is not accompanied by action, is dead.
18 But someone will say, "You have faith; I have deeds." Show me your faith without deeds, and I will show you my faith by my deeds.
19 You believe that there is one God. Good! Even the demons

believe that—and shudder.
20 You foolish person, do you want evidence that faith without
deeds is useless?
James 2:17-20 (NIV)

Reading the Bible is an internal pursuit, whereas action is external. God is our teacher and uses the Scriptures to coach us. His desire for us is to convert this knowledge into actions in the areas that He has in mind.

There is no use of going to university to study medicine and then, after receiving the honours, starting out as an engineer. We need to apply and pursue what we are learning in real life. In chapter "God given Gifts and Talents" we learnt that we are all unique. The Bible guides us how to apply these abilities and urges us to be proactive.

God will never ask you to do anything that you are not capable of. Even if at times it may appear impossible, just go ahead. Have faith, trust and all is well. You will feel it in your heart and you'll enjoy a fulfilled and happy life, free of insecurities, self doubt and fear. Whatever your calling is, may it be teaching, healing, discipling, praying for others, preaching, volunteer work, give financial support or missionary engagements at home or abroad, you will find out.

So, take a leap of faith and go out there to help others to get there too. God doesn't choose perfect people to work for His Kingdom, he chooses the right people. The apostles are a great example: ordinary fishermen, a despised tax collector, a doctor and a feared prosecutor of Christians. God chooses people whose heart is right, not by what they have done in the past or what their experiences are.

What is perfection and how do we define it? What we may consider perfect may not necessarily be perfect in God's eyes. All we need to focus on is to be perfect according to God's standards, He has created you just the way you are: perfect!

Never be surprised when you get a prompting to do something that you have little knowledge of. If this is what God is asking you to do, go ahead. He will provide you with everything you need. Most of all, He will make sure that you will have the right people around you. We are not meant to do life alone. Jesus told His disciples to go out in pairs. We have more strength as a group than as one:

"For where two or three gather in my name, there am I (Jesus) with them."
Matthew 18:20 (NIV)

The same applies when people get together in big crowds to pray. The prayers are much more powerful and many miraculous wonders can occur. There is "more God" when a group of followers gathers in His name.

At times, we may get tempted to coerce others because we are so excited. Pressure will never lead anyone to Christ; we will only scare people away. God never uses force, just follow Jesus' example. Tell them and if they are disinterested, leave it be. It is everyone's own choice. They are not saying *no* to you, they are saying *no* to God. In other words, never take it personally. In the end, God will fight His own war.

14 If anyone will not welcome you or listen to your words, leave that home or town and shake the dust off your feet.
Matthew 10:14 (NIV)

My prayer:

I pray that this book has found you with an open heart. I dare to hope that my interpretations, personal stories, messages, pictures and Bible verses have resonated with you. I know that it is not a coincidence that this book 'fell' into your hands; God led you to it.
I pray in the name of Jesus that the word 'GOD' no longer causes any confusion; rather, evokes love, great inspiration, self confidence and inner peace to go forward with hope in your heart and to share with others.
Amen.

A famous quote by American Evangelist **Hal Lindsay**:

"Human beings can live for <u>forty days</u> without food, <u>four days</u> without water, and <u>four minutes</u> without air. But we cannot live for <u>four seconds</u> without hope."

In times when you encounter confusion, feeling disconnected or vulnerable, read this poem/prayer a few times. You will begin to feel the power of God rise within you. Read it with an open heart and allow the love of God to fill your whole being with renewed strength and courage:

"What name is worthy to be shouted from
the roof tops
what name is eternal
what name is greater
what name is more exalted
and what name can give me greater strength
GOD, your name is matchless

Whose name is love
whose name can be cherished more
whose name has conquered death
whose name can give hope to all
whose name is more powerful
whose name has an echo that never fades
JESUS, your name I love

What other name deserves greater adoration
what other name does my soul yearn for
what other name endures all ages
what other name will I proclaim from the roof tops
with my lungs filled with Your Spirit
GOD, forever I will shout your name"

Amen – Monica

Which points right back to the core of the
apple…God, our Hope and Eternal Refuge

Heaven

Where is Heaven I ask?
And God answers me:

Come to Me
Can you hear Me?
Can you see My Light?
Can you feel My Love?
You can come to Me

Now Heaven is so close
And my soul answers:

Yes my Lord, I am here
My heart sings your praises
Jesus take me by Your hand,
And lead me to Heaven
Yes Lord Jesus, I'm here

I have found Heaven
And my soul sings:

By Your Word I live
Your Spirit I breathe
Your Power is my refuge
Your Name is my salvation
By Your Word I'm healed

Monica M Rohrer 10.06.2016

Footnote:

Four days before I published "Why - Us Against God?" as an e-book, I felt an overwhelming desire to write a poem. At the start, I thought it was going to be something that I could use for another occasion some time in the future. But then I began to realise that "**Heaven**" was meant for this book. God's wants you to know that He is right here. All you need to do is ask and He will answer. These are God's closing words to you: He wants you to be in His presence (Heaven).

Truly, God (Heaven) is closer than you think. I promise that He will change your life as He changed mine. You can experience Heaven right here on Earth. Only God can quench the thirst of your yearning soul.

WHY – Us against God?

June 2016   *published as e-book*

October 2016   *published as Paperback*

June 2017   *revised edition*